It Is
How One Looks at It

by E. C.

It Is
How One Looks at It

by E. C.

EUGENE ST MARTIN JR

IT IS HOW ONE LOOKS AT IT BY E. C.

iUniverse books may be ordered through booksellers or by contacting:

iUniverse
1663 Liberty Drive
Bloomington, IN 47403
www.iuniverse.com
1-800-Authors (1-800-288-4677)

ISBN: 978-1-5320-5597-3 (sc)
ISBN: 978-1-5320-5598-0 (e)

Library of Congress Control Number: 2018909672

Print information available on the last page.

iUniverse rev. date: 08/15/2018

This book is dedicated to my family, friends, and to all the people who have helped me in my life. It is particularly dedicated to my doctors, priests, teachers, students, fellow workers, and fellow players. It is dedicated to all the people I have worked with and for. There is special thanks to Dale Taylor, Alternative Clerical Solutions, the workers at Fed-Ex, and to all the workers at iUniverse. Thank you.

E. C.

Contents

References

Kornfield, Jack. Buddha's Little Instruction Book.
New York, New York: Bantam Books, 1994

Mitchell, Stephen. Tao Te Ching, A New English Version with
Forward and Notes.
New York, New York: Harper and Row, 1988

The New American Bible. Nashville, Tenn.: Thomas Nelson
Publishers, Inc., 1987

CHAPTER
One

STORY #1...seeing the Beauty

The Old Maintenance Man, Groundskeeper

Once upon a time, there was an old maintenance man for some tennis courts at an old country club. Now this maintenance man, he had a lot of resentment inside of him; a lot of anger, a lot of self-doubt and negativism, and a lot of fear. Sometimes, he resented and he was so angry that here he was, a maintenance man, and there this person was teaching tennis, his boss, a tennis pro. That person could get to play tennis and teach tennis, and here I am relegated to sweeping and cutting and fixing this machine, this lawnmower; this lawnmower, which I know so very little about; how to fix a lawnmower! And, sweeping the bathrooms. He was very angry; so much anger that it crawled up inside his skin, at times it made his arm itch.

Now this maintenance man, he liked tennis, he loved tennis. He played tennis himself. Though he didn't really have as much playing skills as his boss, but he too played tennis. It was as if he was stuck, he had him a dead-end job; he was the maintenance man. He was in charge of taking care of the courts and taking care of the grounds around the courts and the building; a groundskeeper. Setting the courts up for people to come and play tennis and then picking up the pieces after they have gone, mending the courts, and helping get them ready for the next day.

Now this maintenance man had a stroke of good luck. He found an old Chinese book written years before Christ was born. He had started reading this book. Some of the words and the ideas in this book really grabbed ahold of this young man, this maintenance man, really caught his attention. And about the same time, he met a very wonderful Chinese couple who introduced him to another couple, a Polish couple, people who enjoyed talking and listening to each other. People who almost made you feel special by listening to you and talking to you.

But what he began to find out as he woke up this next day, after he had met with these couples and after he had read his

Chinese book; he began to see that possibly, right where he was, to see the beauty in right where he was in his life, that there's some reason for him where he is in his life, some reason why he's a maintenance man, a groundskeeper. *There's some reason that God has got me there*, and to just accept it and to go and to take care of the things that he does have in life; that which he does have, the little things that he has. Rather than wanting something else, to take care of the things that he has in his life.

So, this maintenance man, this groundskeeper, he began to get his eye back on the ball, his eye back on the task at hand. Whether that would be taking care of the grounds and the tennis courts or taking care of him. He began to get his eye on his own bagel, also, on his own shape and conditioning. The maintenance man began to go to bed early. He began to start looking at the food he was eating and changing it to a little bit healthier food. He began to walk more, to play tennis. As, he went around his rounds in his life, his most important thing to him was to be loyal to those people right before him, to be loyal to the moment.

As he went around in the rounds of his life, whether he was eating breakfast in the morning at the Country Corner or going to the old Country Club. In all the different dimensions of his life, to be loyal to those people who were right in front of him, to be loyal to himself, to be loyal to the moment.This is what the maintenance man began to do. In his tennis, he began to focus more on the endeavor at hand, to focus on getting that ball back over the net and in play, to putting the ball in play and keeping it in play. For the maintenance man, he began to see tennis as a game of playing in the moment; *this ball coming at me right now this moment*, and *what I'm doing with this ball*. He began to ask himself how he'd *choose to play this game, in what manner did he'd choose to play this game*, and *how to play it in such a way* *that he would refrain from tearing down another player.* Instead, to focus on the ball and what he does with the ball.

He realized that a lot of tennis is overcoming one's own temper, to overcome adversity. And at the end of the game, to shake hands, to have a racket shake, and the game is over with. For as the game may start with love, as it does, it finishes with the word, 'game'.

"What is important to me?" the maintenance man said, "When I look back on my life at the end of my life, and I look at my life and how I lived my life, how do I want to live? How do I want to see myself and what I did during my life?" He thought, "*It's too precious. Life is too precious to go around angry and resentful and negative. Life is too short for that.*"

So, on this particular day, the maintenance man, the old groundskeeper, began to see the beauty that he had, the things that he had, as he went about his rounds that day. And he began to hear the music of the universe that day, the music of God, and to be able to see for a moment, that strand, that thread of God in our world; it's been there all the time. The music's been playing all the time. The beauty's been there all the time. It's always there for those who can see and hear.

CHAPTER
One

STORY #2...*tending to that*

The Old Maintenance Man, Groundskeeper

Once upon a time, there was this old groundskeeper/ maintenance man, and he took care of some tennis courts at an old country club. He played tennis himself. He was beginning to feel bad about himself, his own self-worth, this maintenance man. So, he got to thinking about it and he got himself quiet. He just sat down and looked, watched the trees, the plants, the grass. It was lunchtime and he was watching the Tennis Shop, while everybody else went to go eat. He stayed there to watch the Shop and to answer the phone.

On this particular day, he looked out of the window. He got very quiet and he just looked to see how the trees grew and how the plants grew, and just watched the nature that was going on outside of that window. He began to think and to add some things up. He began to think that, *if you base all your self-worth on what someone says to you, or how someone categorizes you, then you're lost.* Or *if you base all of your actions; and the whole purpose of all of your actions and work is to get admiration, forget it; it never comes.* Or *if a person bases all of his self-worth on whether he wins a tennis match, or he makes "x" amount of dollars;* the maintenance man thought, *"You will feel bad."* **And he thought if you base all of your self-worth on whether someone's going to promote you or not, you know the organization that you work for, the company that you work for, he said** "Forget it, because they're not going to a lot of the times, and then you're going to feel bad."

So, the maintenance man got to thinking some more and he got to thinking about the end of life; the end of his life. And he pictured himself going before God; and what did He say? God asked him, "Did you serve mankind? Did you serve the world? Did you serve the Universe?" And furthermore, God asked him, "Did you love when you were living? Did you live life? Did you learn to let go of all the control and trying to control everything?" So, these are some thoughts in this maintenance man's mind. This was a picture he had of himself going before God; some of the things that God would ask him at the end of his life.

So, the maintenance man began to look back over his life and to rethink his life. He had always wanted some type of a sustaining interest in life – something beyond the dollars and cents. You know tennis; it's a game for life, a game to enjoy life, a game to play throughout one's life. He got to asking some more questions of himself such as, you know, *"How do plants grow? How can I help develop the plants in my yard or the plants in my heart from the ground up – from the seed up?"*

He wondered if it was possible to plant such plants in his life and in his yard. Then, instead of always having a quick fix, importing of a brand new plant already growing, is it possible to start with the young one and help it grow and develop? Oh yeah, I know what it takes to stay on top of it, to follow through. He wasn't use to following through. He needed to learn to follow through; to keep watering it, to keep watching it, keep working with it.

The maintenance man started thinking about his life and what were the things that were fun in his life that felt good? When he felt good, what were some of the small things in his life? He knew that when he sewed on a button he felt good. When he washed his car he felt good. When he raked leaves, there were times when he felt good. When he drew he felt good. And when he took walks he felt good. These are some things that helped and that he enjoyed.

And he began to look and see, *"How could his mind and body work together? How could there be a unified force? What were some of the things that would help him so his mind and body worked together on the task at hand?"* He found out that when he quieted some of the advice inside, some of the chatter inside, when he listened to his breathing and was quieter, his mind and body could work

FIELDS OF SOLITUDE

together; they could be very focused and steady. Because that was one of the most important things in his life, to be steady like a rock, to be steady like a tree, a willow tree that just blows by the wind and comes back, to be very centered, very connected to earth. And that was something that was very important in this maintenance man's life.

So, he began to change. He began to go to bed early, to take better care of himself, to watch the food that he was eating. But most of all, to cherish that which he had in his life: the moments and the people in his life. To love what he had and to love what he does. It wasn't easy. It never is. He still has some of his anger and resentment, but this old maintenance man began to get back on track and he began to love again; and this time, to love everyone.

So, the old maintenance man began to go about his rounds in his life taking care of that which he came upon, taking care of the people who he came upon. And he did this because of caring for that person. And instead of doing it in order to get a raise or to get a promotion, to get someone's attention, to get someone's love; he began to do it for that person, for that thing, for the job, to take care of that which is right in front of him, to tend to that which is right in front of him.

STORY #3...with love

The Old Maintenance Man, Groundskeeper

Once upon a time, there was an old groundskeeper, his name was E. C., and he was beginning to get old and broken down. His neck was beginning to hurt, he already had tennis elbow; and his posture, he knew his posture was no good, it was all bent over. When he went into certain situations he was very tight, very tense; when he held a pencil or a pen he would squeeze too hard. He was having tennis elbow all the time, always changing rackets trying to find the right racket that fit him. He also had this idea that he had to perform. He got very, very nervous before his classes that he taught in the evenings. This groundskeeper would teach tennis in the parks and he would be very nervous before his classes.

Even in the morning to get going; it was very hard for him just to get out of bed. It was always this fear, this self-doubt; how to get his body moving, how to focus on what he was doing. Well, what he began to find out was he began to look at his fear, and his fear it seemed to be, one of the biggest fears was that he himself would fail; that he would fall flat on his face in his classes, it was that he would fall on his face. He began to look at his classes differently and to see them as more of helping the person, working with the person to help this person come up with his/ her own strokes. He began to see his classes where he would be on his knees feeding balls, working with them. Instead of a performance, but to work with them, to help them to find their strokes, to help them to find solutions to this game; that together they would work out solutions for the game, and that it would be a game. Afterwards, at the end of the class, you would shake hands, just as you would shake hands in a regular game, and it would be finished.

Instead of making something a performance, he began to think of going through his life, going through his rounds where he would be tending to that which he had to deal with, that which was right in front of him. To tend to the tasks at hand, to take care of that which was right in front of him; in his case, his grounds keeping duties.

So, this maintenance man began to think and began to feel, and one day he found out, that when lying in bed there; if he could just simply listen to his breathing and breathe in and breathe out; he could focus on his own breathing. To focus on his own bagel the things that he would do, he would be able to get out of bed instead of getting out of bed out of fear. He used to get out of bed because he just wanted to do something for someone. And that was one of the motivations for which he got out of bed. He still did that and he began to find that being able to focus on what he was doing by this breathing, this centeredness, it helped him to move, as opposed to looking down the road too far.

This maintenance man, this old groundskeeper, he wanted something in his life – a thread, a common thread that would, when throughout his whole life that this thread was sacred. He used to have that when he loved someone. He used to have a sense of a thread, a connection to God and to that person, that girl and so forth. And he was looking to get that thread going again.

As he was going in his day, in his rounds and taking care of the tennis courts, he sat down one day, sat on that bench by his shed and just looked; he looked at the trees, looked at the skies, and he got quiet. He saw how the trees were; he saw how the sky was. He began to think about himself and some of the things that he would like to do in his life, to change his posture, to change the way he eats, to change his spirit to be a spirit of joy, to change his attitude. He came up with an idea that there is so much today competing for our attention, there are so many things competing for our attention today, for our time and for our money. If we could just maybe take half of that; our lives, the things that we're trying to do, to just cut it in half and focus on a few things and do those things well or stay with those things. That there's just so much out there competing for our attention; whether it's through the TV, the advertisements, a way of life, so many more activities, we think we can do it all.

In his play, he wanted to change his way of playing tennis; he had been playing for attention before. Some people play for glory, some people play for money, and some people play for the pleasure of playing. And he wanted to go for that or at least, if nothing else, to know what he's playing for and to play for it. But he would like to play for the sake of playing, for the joy of playing in his play.

So, what he was working on was working on finding a way where his body and his mind were working together, that they feel more connected; connected to Earth, connected to the moment and connected to a higher Cause or a person. The old maintenance man began to think that it was better to live in peace. It was better to refrain from asking for anything. It was better to be humble and to love all people. He began to realize that in the game of tennis and in the game of life, that each day is different. Each day the tennis stroke, the angle of the racket is different; it changes each day. One day we are hitting the ball a certain way and another day we're hitting it another way. And how do we make that adjustment in our game? That's the key; that there is every day a change. And that's something that does exist. So the key thing is how to make those adjustments.

He began to learn that tennis is about playing in the moment, this one moment, this ball coming at me right now. He began to even look at the tennis racket and see the circle of the strings and the racket frame in thinking of the moment right now. So that whenever his mind wanders from this moment he could go back to the strings and go back to this circle, this tennis racket circle, and get himself back into this moment. It's about living in the moment. It's about facing the moment. It's facing me now.

For while we change from moment to moment; life is a process of getting it and losing it, arriving and journeying on. About the time we think we're there, we've got it, but then we lose, we want to go to the next step or life changes. So, he began to think of his tennis teaching like that and finding ways that he could help people to make that adjustment. Would he just be a person who would set people straight? Force in a lot of ideas, a lot of his own ideas, his own style? Or, would he be a guide along the highway? Would there be some way that they could set up a way in which they could find their own way, their own path? In this case, the tennis ball traveling a certain path; or playing a certain game. How to set up parameters so that the person can figure out what's going on in this match, and how I can play this match; that's what it's about, this game of tennis, this game of teaching, this game of coaching, so that person can make their adjustments on their own.

He found that, for himself, it helped to quiet his mind and to listen to his breathing. It helped also to see where the ball goes in relation to his target. He found also that it helped the non-racket hand and the brain helped make that adjustment. So, it boils down in a way, how to use our minds to make that adjustment, to figure out what's going on with our shots, and what's going on in the overall pattern of play.

The old maintenance man, yes, he was stuck, but he wanted to change. He wanted to come up with a thread in his life where he would truly, simply get out of bed that day and find a connection through a higher purpose throughout his whole life; a connection, connection to God, connection to nature, a connection to the people in his life, connection to what he's doing. And that is what he's doing; he's doing it in a good manner in love for that person. As he goes along his journey, that life, that day, that he's being a helping hand, helping here and helping there in a real way. And that he's playing some himself; that he's got his eye on his bagel, on his doughnut, the cleaning up of his car, of his house, the playing of his game also, as well as the respect for the other person.

CHAPTER
One

STORY #4... *a direction*

The Old Maintenance Man, Groundskeeper

Once upon a time, there was an old maintenance man. He was a groundskeeper for the tennis courts at an old country club and he was beginning to get a bit broken down. This maintenance man also used to teach tennis in the evenings in the parks. He was coming upon a time in his life when he was beginning to look at himself, to look in the mirror and begin to ask some questions about his life.

It came down to this; he was beginning to want to be going towards something. Whether it was nature or family or tennis, he needed to rethink his ways of teaching tennis. For him, life was becoming too short. It was too short to start endeavors halfway. It was better for him, he thought, to take a few things through to the finish and to stick with them. A few things like teaching tennis and visiting a friend, like drawing and writing. But this was the time when he began to look into the mirror and to look into his own soul. For at this time of his life, he needed to make a commitment, he needed to dig in. And that's what this old maintenance man was beginning to do.

He wanted to go towards something, towards building something, to be going towards something; the discovery of nature, to participate himself in the great mystery, the great mystery of the world. These were some of the things that he would like to do. He knew that so much of his problem was being able to keep his eye on the task at hand, to take something through to the finish. There are different ways to accomplish this. But for him, he needed to find a very basic natural way to do this, where he became focused, where he would help take something through to the finish. To take a moment and to spend time talking with a person, to complete something, to compete a task, to do it all the way through to the finish. And in his life he knew that he needed to do this within himself, without overextending himself;

overspending his energy or his money or his time. He was only one person and he could just do so much.

So, he began to think about his tennis teaching and he began to think about his work, about focusing on the task at hand and staying out of people's feelings. Sometimes the relationships come as a byproduct of the work together; where two people keep their eye on the ball, the ball of getting the courts ready for people to come play tennis. **The ball; the ball in tennis, of getting this ball over the net and in bounds.** Where I get my ball over and in bounds and then the other person gets it over and in bounds. And then when we can, we place it away from our opponents just out of their reach. And they do what they can to place it away from us just out of our reach. Each person is focusing on their own ball. Each person's focusing on the overall whole, too. And as a byproduct of all this, there'll be different feelings and relationships and all of this sort of stuff. But the main task at hand is putting this ball in play and keeping it in play.

So, the old maintenance man wanted, and knew he needed to work on his attitude, on changing his attitude, on changing his anger, his resentment. He needed to sit down for a minute and figure out, *"Hey, just what is important to me?"* And he needed to stick with it. In teaching tennis he began to think, *"There needs to be a way to learn and a way to teach. And it's a game, it's about playing games and it's about understanding people."* He needed to look at it from the point of view of the student, from the point of view of the teacher, from the point of view of the different people around; the people playing next door and the park itself. But overall, there needs to be a way to learn and a way to teach.

The old maintenance man began to think about his own tennis game and how he played tennis as far as in competition. And in competition, this maintenance man, this tennis player, often gave himself the short end of the stick. In a match, maybe one should refrain from giving oneself the short end of the stick. And people who were the winners, I guess in the score, they refrained from giving themselves the short end of the stick. Maybe this maintenance man did it just so people would like him, so they would like him.

But possibly a match is different from that; a match is a competition. Each person giving themselves the long end of the stick, and hopefully giving the other person the short end of the stick. And in a cooperative manner, yes, you do sometimes give yourself the short end of the stick for the other person; you do look after the other person, you put them before you. It's really something, isn't it? No one needs to give the short end of the stick in order to get love, 'cause it doesn't ever happen that way. You need to just give the short end of the stick to the other person because you love them in and of themselves, because you love them and you expect nothing back in return.

So, the maintenance man began to think about teaching tennis in terms of how he would like to hit the ball, and in terms of how he would like to be treated. He began thinking about the teaching of tennis and how to set up an environment where people can learn, where people can have fun, and where it prepares them for the game. He began to look at his work and his personal life as being more supportive of other people, the people with whom he comes in contact each day. And to begin to see nature, to draw nature, to write, to have an interest in life, a significant interest in the way life is.

And the old maintenance man began to think about teaching and coaching as a service. Is what he is doing a service to others? That's the key; whether his lesson is a service to others, whether his work is a service to others. And to focus on that, and to focus on doing the little things that come up each day that draw his attention, that grab him, that gnaw at him to be fixed, to be completed, to be picked up, to be done. Those little bitty things that grab his attention, the things that are asked each day, the little bitty things. And that his work overall is a service rather than trying to be the boss or the one in control; that was more the direction he wanted to go, he needed to go. He needed to work for and to work towards.

CHAPTER
One

STORY #5...
seeing a single flower

The Old Maintenance Man, Groundskeeper

*T*hat his work and his teaching, is it a service to that person? He knows that's it in the little bitty things. The little things in how he does his work and how he does his teaching and how he plays tennis. And he knows it's in how we participate with nature, how we participate with the universe, with the great mystery that's unfolding; and that, are we participating with this Mystery, this great mission? Are we listening to the song that's being sung? Are we seeing the beauty that's out there? Regardless of whether we hear it or not, there's a song that's being sung, there's a beauty out there in this world. And to hear that, hear that song; see that beauty; that's what it's about.

So, the old maintenance man, a tennis teacher and tennis player, he began to see if what he does in life brings life. If what he does, is it connected to life, is it a service? Is it possibly that tennis is putting a ball in play, serving a ball, and keeping that ball in play over the net and in the court? Oh yes! And when we can, to place it away from our opponents. But the first thing is to put that ball in play and keep that ball in play.

And then, there's the idea where you know, Christ – His idea, what He did – where He picked up that cross that He had and He carried that cross. He faced that obstacle that He had, that moment that He had right in front of Him, and He did it. The task that He had that was facing Him; He picked it up and carried it. And that's actually what He was wanting us to do, if we choose, to pick up our own cross and to follow Him. To follow the ways that He did, the ways that He lived. To pick up our own cross, that which is facing us – each one of us has our own cross – and to follow in a manner like Christ. Each one of us is on a journey. Every one of us has our own journey.

Hey, the purpose is that which is leading to God; and that's really what it's about, leading to God; our journey. And along our way we cross each other's paths or we walk with each other.

Sometimes we help each other. Sometimes we walk along and talk and share ideas, and sometimes we walk and talk and don't say anything, and sometimes we walk and go away from each other and come back and tell what we saw. And our paths cross different ways; and some people take this path and other people take this other path. Still there's an overall direction, an overall source in which everything is going. Whether we like it or not, we're going towards a source.

And the old maintenance man, he thought, "*Well what about a wife; if there was any chance to have a wife, what would be important to him?*" And for him, he thought it would be someone to talk to and someone to talk with; hopefully someone that he could work with. That they could work with each other without having to force it. And that's basically what he would like, someone to hold and to hug and to kiss. Sure, he would like some nourishment, some emotional and spiritual nourishment, but he needs to give, too; he needs to give some in return.

So, the old maintenance man was beginning to think, "*You know, my deal is to take care of my people, to remember my people, and to play whatever game there is. But the main game of teaching is teaching and coaching; and the main game of playing is playing, and to stick to the overt games. And to remember who one's people are.*" Although, really in real life, our people are all our people that we come in contact with as we make our rounds in life, as we hear about other people and that we hold them in our heart.

So, the old maintenance man, a tennis teacher and tennis player; one day he was sitting in the shop watching the shop while everybody was eating and he looked through a little book. It was a little book on Buddhist ideas, well on ideas from Buddha; a little simple book. It was a beautiful book with beautiful pictures and with just one thought, one idea on each page, a beautifully drawn book; very simple, condensed ideas from Buddha. And these are what some of the ideas said, "In the end these things matter most: How well did you love? How fully did you live? How deeply did you learn to let go?" And another page said, "We do not possess our home or our children or even our body; they are only given to us for a short while, to treat with care and respect." And that maintenance man thought, "*So, to our friends.*" And another page said, "If you take care of each moment, you will take care of all time." And further, the maintenance man, as he flipped through the pages and looked, and he looked out the window, and he looked at the trees and the shrubs and the bees and the flowers and the grass, he read this, "If we could see the miracle of a single flower clearly, our whole life would change."

It seemed to be what the maintenance man started doing. He started to go and to look at the flowers and see how they grew, and the plants and how they grew. Whenever he had problems he began to go and consult the trees, consult the grass, consult the flowers, the birds, just to see how they live. Later on, the maintenance man looked again in that little book, and this is what he found on the page as he opened the book. This was the page that, as he just randomly opened the book, this was what was on the page. It said, "See for yourself what brings contentment, clarity and peace. That is the path for you to follow."

The old maintenance man, a tennis teacher and tennis player, began to become a little bit more focused, a little bit quieter as he went through his life. He stopped his preaching. He simply began to serve, to work, to take care of that which came his way.

CHAPTER

One

STORY #6... *the endeavor at hand*

The Old Maintenance Man, Groundskeeper

Once upon a time there was an old maintenance man, a groundskeeper of the tennis courts at an old country club, and he was a tennis teacher in the evenings. It was kind of like a Zorro act; in the daytime he had this job, in the evening he'd change clothes and got into another job. But he began to think about himself and his life, and he knew he had a nervous condition, a significant nervous condition. Early in his life he had been diagnosed as having this, and he knew this.

So one day, though, he was still fighting it and talking about it in his mind, debating it. Sometimes the condition had been called this, or sometimes it had been called that, or been called something else, or it was a bunch of them all. But he remembered, as he walked down the street, he remembered a story; it was a story about a man who was a TV actor. And, this man had this variety show on TV.

The man was described as a nervous person. But the one thing about the actor; he always did his job. **No matter** how nervous he was; always, the show went on. And so he began to say, *"Hey look,"* the maintenance man, *"that there, there is a show that goes on, there is an endeavor that goes on."* **And whether I have my nervous condition or not, I need to work to take care that that show goes on, that that endeavor goes on.**

So he began to think, the maintenance man, he began to think and he thought, *"What are the things that I do have? The body that I do have, the biology that I do have. What are my givens? The things that I have, and to use what I do have."* And he began to say and to think, *"You know I can watch what I eat, that's something I can do. I can watch what time I go to bed, that's another thing that I can do for myself. And my exercise, I can be more active or I can exercise in a very creative manner."*

Oh yeah, each day is different. Each day as we wake up, we have a different angle on the tennis racket – so to speak – we hit the ball this way or we hit the ball that way; but how to make those adjustments? And the maintenance man began to say, "*You know, I can begin to talk about myself rather than talking about the other person or thinking about what they're doing. Yes, I need to be aware, but I can still focus on my actions more, on the things I do; on my bagel. And I can live within my means more. I can start watching the money I'm spending and the time I'm spending and the attention I'm spending to certain things.*"

And the maintenance man began to think, and the old man, he began to think, "*You know, one idea is to give no grief to anyone, to really watch what I say to others; the comments. And when I get stressed, instead of going and getting a Coca-Cola all the time,* he said, "*I know, I can sit down and drink some water and be quiet, and I can take a few more naps when I get really tired. And you know, there's one thing I can do all the time, if I choose, and that's to watch my posture; I can work on my posture for a year. And when it's time to play a game — hey, play the game; play the real game at hand. Stick to that, rather than the side games. Stick to the work, rather than the side games. Stick to the teaching and the listening and the guiding, rather than the side games. And when the lesson's over with, pick the balls up, shake hands or have a racket shake and say, 'Thank you!' for sharing this time with me, for being willing to share this little bit of your time with me.*"

So, the maintenance man began to think, "*Oh yes, okay, all right I've got a nervous condition; that's what I've got; that's a given.*" But still there is an overall task going on, an overall endeavor; still the Universe is functioning, it's going on. And if I choose, I can help put my might behind that Universe, the functioning of that Universe, the task at hand. I can put my might, that which I do have, behind helping to get this ball over the net and inbounds. And that's all, that's all there is.

Then there's another time a person can pick their ball up and send it back over, if they choose. For teaching it means, hey, to help prepare those people, those students for the match, for the game; so that they all have a chance to play, too; to participate in this game. That they all can play and have a chance to play in the match.

So, the old maintenance man began to live within himself. He began to refrain from putting something over on another person. Instead, he simply lent a hand, he helped, and he gave his hand and his heart to the endeavor at hand. He began to see what God was doing in the Universe. He began to see the forces of nature; he began to act in accord to them, and to that. Instead of setting the world straight; he began to set himself straight, in accord to the way things go and the way things are, and to what God wanted, to God's plan.

Oh, and yes! Sometimes he even, if he was lucky, would make a drawing of the things that were in the world; the beauty, the songs that were being sung.

CHAPTER
One

STORY #7...to stop
and look at the rain

The Old Maintenance Man, Groundskeeper

Once upon a time there was this old maintenance man, this old groundskeeper at an old country club. And this groundskeeper used to take care of the tennis courts and he also used to teach tennis in the evenings in the parks. He'd come there for a tennis job – so he thought – so he possibly could work his way up to be tennis pro, or to go somewhere else to become a tennis pro. He had gone on a trip, a wonderful trip to New York to learn about teaching tennis, and to see New York City, to see the people and see how everybody moves and acts, and to enjoy the different people of New York City; and he had come back.

When he came back from his vacation, here he was again; he seemed to be stuck again, the same old place. He was doing the maintenance and the other person, the tennis pro, was doing the tennis teaching. And this man became more angry at himself and angry at this tennis teacher – the pro – his boss, and everybody else there. It was as if he was stuck. Here he is cleaning the bathrooms, sweeping the walks, repairing the lawn mowers, and this other person is doing the tennis teaching and having all the fun.

So, he was really stuck until he began to think. And he was fortunate to come upon some different people who treated him with respect and with interest, and this helped. He enjoyed teaching tennis in the place where he had taught tennis – he was the tennis pro, he was the tennis teacher. But he still needed to look at his own life and to see what he could do for his life; that there must be some reason that this is the place where he is at this moment. That there is some reason he's at this moment and at this place. And this is his place and the tennis pro, that's his place; and they have two different places. And there's some reason why they're in different places at that moment for their lives and for maybe each other's lives and for other people around them.

After all, that's the reason he should be there. He's there to help work for the people at that club, regardless in whatever capacity.

So the old tennis player, the old tennis pro – no, really the old maintenance man, the groundskeeper; he began to look at his life and to see what he could do with what he had, to do something about where he is. And one thing was that, he could do the work that he does, he could do it in a caring manner. He could take care of what he's doing without putting something over on another person, without trying to hoodwink someone. Or do it for the boss or do it for attention, but do it because of the job; and to take care of it. Nothing too fast, nothing too slow; simply take care of what he's doing.

And in this teaching of tennis in his own life; a total commitment. It takes a total commitment; a total commitment to his job, a total commitment to his life; to life itself. And that was really what the maintenance man was after, a consistency, firmness, a steadiness to life, something that would be of an interest, almost a sustaining interest throughout his whole life, so that he would live his life out. No checking out of life. No checking out of the game, to finish the game.

He began to see how the trees worked. Just how do trees grow and live and breathe; and the foundation of the trees. He began to look at a perspective of life from the point of view of the tree, and the flowers, and the plants. And sometimes when he had troubles, he would go consult a tree and just go see how they grow and how they live with where they are.

The old maintenance man began to see each person; how there was some beauty in each person. Each person has a different name. Each person has their own beauty when you look at them in a way that is non-judgmental. When you look at them in the way that an artist looks at a person, you'd begin to see the beauty of each person. In his teaching, he began to see, to look for ways in which he could set up a learning environment different from setting the people straight; but a way that they could learn in a shared way, a shared mission.

The old man began to look and feel the rhythm of his work. And in his sweeping, and his walking, and pushing of the wheelbarrow, to see the beauty of that rhythm; to experience the rhythm of swinging in the tennis racket, of sweeping with the broom. He knew that in tennis some of the very best players; they really went for their shots. This Steffi Grafts, she really went for her shots, she was aiming for something.

And the old maintenance man, he wanted to have the ability someday to talk with a person, to be able to focus his whole attention on that conversation with that person and to be free to do it and willing to do it. That seems to be one of the hardest things for him; the willingness to let go of what he wanted to do instead of listening to that person and giving full attention to that person.

The old maintenance man began to realize that there was no need for him to get so stressed out. To set up a situation where he's so stressed out, that he's so tense, that he's so tight or even a sense that he is performing. Or maybe just to go about it as he is tending to the task at hand, tending to that which is right in front of him. Whether that is a person's tennis stroke or whether that is the trash or the leaves to pick up or the tennis court to get ready so that other people can come; and to play and to learn and to enjoy.

He was beginning to realize it takes a total commitment. It takes digging deep down inside of oneself, one's motivation. And to ask oneself, *what is one's motivation? What does one care about? Who does one care about? Is it always just about control and becoming 'Mr. Control', being the boss?* It was so hard for that man, that old maintenance man, to take orders, for someone else to be in control of him; it was so hard. And yet sometimes he tried to control others himself. He always loved to be in control. Maybe he could learn how to trust instead; maybe he could learn that it's not a matter of control. It's more like being like the tree blowing with the wind or like the water flowing, hitting a rock, going around the rock. Or it's more of looking at the overall picture, the bigger picture, and going with the flow towards the bigger picture; because that's what's really happening. To stop a moment and to see the beauty that is happening, that is unfolding.

The maintenance man used to love to stop and see the rain. He loved it when it rained, because it meant that his activities could stop for a moment. And once in a while, he would just stop and look at the rain, the drops falling on the other puddles and those little rings going out, concentric rings traveling out from the center of that little drop; oh the rain! It's a time to stop and just look.

CHAPTER
One

STORY #8...the symphony

The Old Maintenance Man, Groundskeeper

G ood morning! It's morning time. I know I need to get going. Here I am in this bed. When I look down the road too much; I never get out of bed. It's better to just go back to breathing in and out, to wake up, and to get out of this bed. And it helps for me to have something or someone to get out of bed for; something I want to do, something I want to give to someone that day. That's what helps me early in the morning.

Yes I've got a nervous condition; okay, I've got one. Still I can focus on the show that's going on, on the Universe, on the game, on the unfolding of the great mystery; and I can be a part of that. I can help participate in that in my own way, in my little bitty way. There is a task at hand, and in tennis it's that ball; getting that ball over the net and in bounds. Hey, stay out of people's personalities; get this ball over and in bounds. Oh, relationships and stuff, they'll come.

Oh, yes, I'd love to find my niche in this world, to use the talents that I have; gosh that would be great. To be able to be like an artist, or a scientist or a writer, someone who just naturally does this and those talents are good, and it feels good to do them, and it's good for someone else; that would be wonderful. Maybe, for me, it's getting on my knees and teaching tennis. Maybe if I'm lucky it's writing and drawing.

It's still early morning. I think I need to make my early morning simpler; I know I do. I've got too much baggage, too much luggage, too much 'shoulds' and stuff. I do like to face God for a moment. I do like to talk. I do love the exercises. I just simply need to make some of my baggage lighter and simpler. I do need to feed the birds. Okay, I've got a nervous condition. Still I can focus on the overall game. There's no need any more to attract attention. I just simply need to do it and get out of there. I need to look at the water and see how does water run downhill or how water just runs over the land. As you take water and you pour it on the land and just see how it runs, there's nothing perfect. And so, too, there's nothing perfect in the game of tennis, it's a constant adjustment, as far as playing the game. Oh yes, we want to hit our ball and we want to feel good about hitting our ball, find that place, that way that it feels so fun to hit the ball; and that's important. And yet, too, it's a game, it's an adjustment; so, it's both, it's hitting the ball, the how, the manner in which we play, and an overall purpose, an overall objective, the game itself, the person that you're playing; in taking what we have; using the racket that we have, the body that we have, to play that game, and to play the real game, that which is the game.

There's probably no big answers to these things, it's probably in every day little bitty things. Little bitty gnawings and scratchings and things that are brought to our attention and some people are so lucky to do them, to complete them. First you do one, then you do another, and before long when the big thing comes, it's very easy to do, it's easier to do, because you've been doing little bitty things all along. And those little things all along anyhow, mount up to bigger things. It's just like in the game of tennis, every point mounts up to the whole, every point is important. What matters is the point we're facing now, the task we're facing now.

Through it all, there are other people, there's another source of power there's a God. So, we're all together, we're many parts that help make up a whole. So, other than just one person doing it all, we're all together helping to make up this whole symphony of life. When we choose to join into that symphony, thank God; that's where it's at.

CHAPTER
Two

STORY #1...the song

The Old Maintenance Man, Groundskeeper

Once upon a time, there was a young maintenance man for the tennis courts and his name was E. C. And, as time went on, this young man now became an old man, an older man. And, he moved from his job of taking care of the tennis courts to a new job. It was a job working at a Parks and Recreation Department in a beautiful city. He was to look after the tennis teaching, the teaching of the tennis instruction in the city and in the town. Oh, he had been teaching there in this city system for over 22 years, but now he had taken on a full-time job in being involved with the Parks and Recreation Department. And E. C. really didn't have the good attitude about it; he really needed to change his attitude. There was pressure; he felt the pressure, he felt the way things were.

So one day, he began to think about his attitude and began to think about himself, his life and how he had gotten off from what he really used to love to do. He used to love to be outside with nature. He used to love to stop and to see the different flowers, the plants, the trees, and the birds; to stop and talk to people, and listen to people in an easy and informal way. He needed to get back to that. He needed to change his attitude.

Well, one day, he finally started looking at himself in the mirror and determine what he was becoming, the kind of human being he was becoming. And he wanted to change it. He needed to get back to where he was in the sense of how he was before, or how he perceived himself and how he wished he could be. He knows he needs to focus on the task, the task at hand; to getting the ball over the net today, to getting the job done today. He knows he just simply needs to be willing to do the work and to accept himself for who he is. Still he wants to change; he wants to be better, to be healthier, to be fit, to be more genuine with people, and to be loving and caring towards people.

He knows he needs to get his own act together. It's involved with the teaching of tennis or, more particularly, the working with people in the game of tennis, teaching of people, and working with people helping them to find their game, helping them to find their mind, to do it in a positive manner versus taking things away from people. To really sincerely be for the kids rather than for some glory for himself, or some glory by having so many kids who are ranked or good players; to really be for the welfare of the kids at hand; that's what he needed to do. And he needed to get his own life back into a sense of sacredness, where he was living a sacred life, where he was living within himself, and yet, at the same time, he was living within harmony with God and with nature and with the environment.

In his tennis teaching, he began to work on helping people focus on the process of the game, on the playing of the game, versus so much focus on the score and the winning. And so too in his work, he began to think of the process versus the outcome, of the taking care of the little things at his work, helping keep theup before they become emergencies, helping look after the little bitty things like wind screens and sweeping and picking up trash; helping so the place can be playable and safe, and people can flow.

He began to start to walk, and to sweep, and to push and to pull, and to blow the courts, and to talk to people in an easy manner. Then, a funny thing happened; he began to see the beauty of nature again. To see the little joys that are right in front of us and all around us; the birds flying, the clouds in the sky, the flag blowing in the wind, and the beautiful flowers. He began to help take care of where he worked and his own home, and his own friends, as he traveled throughout his life. He began to work to get his mind into the present moment; to focus on the ball coming at him right now and taking care of that shot, to gently bring his mind back into the present moment.

He began to see the opportunity that is right before him, to see the opportunities and to focus on the opportunities, versus the shortcomings, to continually focus on the opportunities that are there; opportunities to do work. And again, the shapes and the colors in the world; he saw them again. He had seen them every day, but now they began to come and have new meaning for him. He wished he could draw again, and he wished he could write, for he began to see and to be connected to something bigger than himself. He wished this with his whole heart; he wished to live in a genuine manner, and sincere manner, and a steady manner. But he knew and he knows that there is something bigger than him, and he wishes and wants to connect with that and flow with that; to simply be God's instrument, to be one with God, to flow with God as God plays the instrument, as God plays him; to be willing to let that song come out.

CHAPTER
Two

STORY #2...wishes

The Old Maintenance Man

E. C. was thinking one day, *"Where do I spend my positive energy, my love? Where do I spend my energy in my thoughts? What do I think about? That defines me that defines who I am. We can change our thoughts."* he thought. *"Still, where do I spend my positive energy, my love?"*

E. C. wished at many times that he could be like a tree that could be flexible and bending. Sometimes he listens to trees just to see how to live. He looks at trees and observes them. How they move with the wind, and how they grow from the ground up, how they give off oxygen to people. How quiet they are at times, and yet at times they make noise, they have their seasons. And then he wondered about reality, *"What really is reality?"* And he thought, *"It's a place where I live now, where I am now; and to focus on that."* To focus on the place where he is and the task that he is doing now. Meanwhile, he can still stop and see the flowers and see the beauty that's in this place right now.

And he thought more about life-supporting and sustaining activities. *"Oh, yes, that's the opportunity to love right now; where I am. To love the place where I am right now and love the people I'm with right now. For where is my attention at this moment? Where is my mind at this moment? Where my mind goes; goes my attention, goes my path; goes my direction."* He really found this in driving the last couple of days. As he thought different thoughts, so too, he drove his car into the wrong parking lot. Often our paths go according to what we are thinking about, and one's own path defines oneself.

And he looked at the birds, and the resourcefulness of the birds; the sparrows in particular. How they're able to adapt to changes; they seemed to get along. And often many, they're simply scratching at a living, finding some food to eat, finding some shelter in rain and cold, keeping warm. There's a lot to be learned from the birds. And he began looking at his tennis matches as a challenge to do his part to make a match. Perhaps he could use some of the resourcefulness of the birds; perhaps he could care for the ball and take responsibility.

He went to a tennis tournament, a very special tennis tournament, a wheelchair tennis tournament. He worked as a water-boy, as a person bringing the water to the courts and helping get the courts ready for play. In this tournament, he did a very special thing. He put his ego on the shelf and he helped as much as he could, and he refrained from talking negatively. A funny thing happened; he had a tremendous experience in the tennis tournament in helping around the tennis tournament. It really was a different life from what he was doing when he was working. Of course, he was volunteering, but still he worked as hard as everybody else, and he just worked to make it be a good experience for everybody. It really turned his whole life around for that particular week; he had different juices flowing inside of him, and he thought that what he was doing was important. One just needs to be willing to toss a ball, like to his friend, Mitch, and to truly serve the students.

E. C. found that as the days went on; although, they were similar days, the meanings changed of each day. There was a change in the perception, his perception, his depth perception, and he longed to get back to that truer depth perception, where he was caring for people, and truly getting involved with caring for people, and forgetting about himself.

The other day E. C. went to Church. And at Church, in his following days, he began to think about some things. One of them is, *"Life is so short! Life is very short. Still, today I'm here. This day I can take care of the things I have today in front of me. I can have courage to take care of this day."* And he thought further, *"Where there's a will; there's a way, to see opportunities today, and see opportunities for the future."*

He knows that he needs to clean up his own act. Oh, and his home is clutter, yes, but also more importantly, in his heart and in his thoughts and in his motivation. He knows he needs to purify his motivation and to keep working on it. He knows he will always be working on that. And he knows he needs to chop the cotton, to tend to the task at hand, that's good, and that's enough. E. C. wished for faith in God and a steadiness. Oh, that was so important for him, it is so important; this steadiness, a basic steadiness in life. Maybe it comes from facing his fear, from facing himself, and from facing that fear and from taking care of the little things in life, and for doing things that are steady; the steadiness will come from having a mind that is steady, this steadiness will come. Refraining from being dependent on other things that are very much out of our control, like computers and machines a lot; this steadiness will come.

When he was in Church that evening he read something from the Bible, it was from the Ephesians (Ephesians 5:15-20) and it went like this: 'When we forsake foolishness in our lives, we go strong in understanding.' It also went on to say, 'To keep a watchful eye on their contact in the way they could overcome their ignorance and discern the will of God.' Yes, E. C. wished to get back to caring for people and back to reality. He thought, *"Maybe I can do something very beautiful for this world. Maybe there's something I can do that is nice for this world, nice for someone, and do something beautiful for this world."*

E. C. also knew that he needs to take the time to be thankful for the people in his life and all the things that are in his life right now. That this is a time to stop, to look into our lives, and to see all the many gifts that have been given to us, so many gifts in our lives; a time to be thankful for the ingredients in the people in our lives now. And from this, carry on in a positive manner, in a caring manner, sticking with people, focusing the mind. Yes, within the lines, within the boundaries. And to see the beauty of each person, to have an artist eye, to see the beauty in each person that comes out, to be non-judgmental, to love my car, to love my home, to love my neighbors, to love my work; for what we do is important.

STORY #3...motivation

The Old Maintenance Man

You know, once upon a time, there was a young man, who was a maintenance man for tennis courts, his name was E. C. And he realized that often he had nothing but grudges and resentments inside of him. He needed to get rid of those and to serve; he knew this. He knew that his life was off balance, and his shoes, his cold, his anger, his mind all were off balance today; instead of being in the present moment and at peace and in breathing. And he realized that how we all live, how we construct our lives, to some extent, is how we live; it's our own heaven or hell. He knows, E. C. knew he needed to get in touch with his own motivation, his true motivation. And he knew he needed to refrain from putting any excessive pressure on his life; life is too short.

E. C. thought, *"You know life was given me, the gift of life, God has given me the gift of life, and I need to give back. I need to give back to life. I need to give back to God. Everything I have is a gift from God."* And E. C. knew that if God is patient with us, he needed to be patient with himself. That night he thought, *"I love thee, God, and thank you, Jesus, for what you have done for me, what you did for me. I know I've not been very reciprocating, but thank you for what you did for me, and I need to understand this more."* E. C. realized.

He asked himself, *"If I could do anything in the world; what would I do?"* And he thought, *"He would write, he would draw, he would help people in the little ways that he could. And he would work to keep himself in balance and to be towards balance, to balance as much as he could, and to become steady as best as he could."* He remembered times when he used to really enjoy serving people and working for people and talking with them. He wished to get back to that. E. C. knew that what he really had, one thing he had was his integrity, and when it boils down in life that's what he has is his own integrity. And he knew that he needed to learn how to use his brain, his mind, both sides, the left side of the mind and the right side of the mind; to use the whole brain.

And he knew that people who followed their interests were lucky people. People who simply loved to hit a tennis ball, because it was interesting to them to hit the tennis ball, to simply play the game, because it was interesting to them to play the game. Different than for praise, or for attention, or to get attention from other people or for accolades or rankings, or to be number one or to be good; but in and of itself, it was an interesting thing to move, to hit the tennis ball, the feel of hitting the tennis ball, of serving the tennis ball, and of playing the game.

E. C. knew that he had lost some of the things that he used to be. He knew that he had never become what he would have loved to be. Though he knows now that he can still shoot for it, because no one ever does become totally what they are to be. It's a process; it's all an ongoing process. He can keep shooting to have an artist eye, and he can shoot to be better at being with people, and taking care of people, and working for people, and listening to people, and being genuine to people. E. C. began thinking about the game of tennis and he began to think about his own mind. He knew now that he needs to be at peace with his own mind, his own condition. And still he knows he needs to keep in shape and to get in shape in order to do the task at hand, to climb that hill in front of him mentally, physically, emotionally and spiritually. He knows he needs to understand the mind that he does have, and to be at peace with that, to be at peace in the moment with which he is in.

So E. C. began to think about tennis and the playing of tennis and one of the things he came up with, he thought that he needed a pure intention, he needed to have a pure intention for playing. To massage the ball, to play the ball; focus on the ball and to place it just out of reach of his opponent; that was a purpose, versus to wow attention. It's more real to play the ball and to play the person. Oh! Stay out of their personality. E. C. knew he needed to bring one's mind to the present, to empty the mind, quieting and see, and to breathe, listening to the breathing, quieting and looking at the trees and the flowers and listening. His goal was to keep his mind in each point. His objective was to eventually place that ball out of reach of his opponent and to stay out of that person's personality. He needed to have his mind in each point and to trust the strokes that he has. He also liked to have a solid shot, a solid hit on the ball.

So, E. C. began to know and to realize that you take the moment that you have and you work with it, with the ingredients that you have; whether you're teaching a person or playing the points in the match, taking the ingredients that one has and to work with it. He also needed to realize, where does he put his attention? Where do we put our attention? He also knew and realized that practice was a chance for this to unfold; to create a place to practice, a chance to unfold. And he also knew that a teacher was really a guide; that a lot of the ingredients were already there and for us to take the ingredients given to us and then turn them into something, something positive.

CHAPTER
Two

STORY #4...*turning it around*

The Old Maintenance Man

Once upon a time there was a tennis teacher who was old and getting old and disgruntled, getting stuck in his ways, a lot of stuck energy. He had taken some time off and he began to think about his life. He wanted to be going to somewhere, he wanted to help build something, to be going somewhere in his life. He wanted to get involved more into the process of teaching and the process of playing versus the pressure of the situation; to organize his life better, to organize the ways of teaching and working and helping others so that the good can come out; that he can be helpful again to other people.

Oh, he was broken down, he was burned out. But he wanted to find a way to teach in a new way and to live in a new way. He knew he needed to focus on the process of the learning and the playing, and on the student, the substance of the student. He wanted to stay away from giving a lot of suggestions and advice to his students. Instead, more, to get on his knees and to feed balls, to help them find their own game, their own strokes, their own game in tennis. So, one idea he had heard was to set up little steps, little stages and exercises where people themselves could learn and to play; that they could come up with the answer themselves. Set up little exercises where people could actually teach themselves and they could come up with the answers. Where it was like a problem-solving, but helping the student themselves solve the problem.

In his own life he wanted and needed to learn how to love his own body, how to love others, and to love God. He needed to love his work again and to take care as one does one's work and teaches one's lessons, and to do it; versus to impress, to get by, or to pull and push too much. He needed to focus on the true things in tennis, and those things, to work with those things, and to play in those dimensions. He had an idea that possibly he could devise certain games together with the students, whereby you play and at the same time you engage them. He had an idea to teach strokes that were good for the whole body and for the whole mind because tennis is played in wholes.

He wanted to know what he was really about, what was important to him. And he thought about some of his students, and he thought of them, the ones he worked with, the ones he gets along with particularly and he realized that's what's important. Oh, he still needed to work on his motivation and his intention and having a pure intention.

Still, the old tennis pro began to love what he did again. He began to love his home more, love the people that he was with, and he began to honor the work/rest ratio. He also knew that part of tennis was teamwork and working together with someone. At the same time, the old tennis teacher knew that he needed to work with his own nerves and with the ingredients that were given to him in his life. And he knows that there'll be times when his nerves and his fears will come into being. But he now knows he needs to face those fears, he needs to work with those ingredients that have been given him, and take those ingredients, turning them into a beautiful meal, a beautiful lesson or a lesson that's a sound lesson. He knew that today he needed to face the ball that's coming at him right now, the one today, the one that is in his court today. He also knows he needs to serve and to return that ball within the dimension that he is in.

CHAPTER
Two

STORY #5...
where is my focus?

The Old Maintenance Man

One time, there was an old broken down tennis teacher, who was sitting and contemplating life, looking out the window at his home, looking at the trees and the birds and the squirrels and thinking about his life. He wished for a life with a sense of purpose. He wished that there was a deep thread throughout his life, that life itself was sacred and everything that he did in his life would be sacred, would be connected to this sacred thread of life, this sacred mission of life or the unfolding of life. Seeing life as it is, seeing the beauty in life, and seeing how the great Mystery unfolds and working with that, being part of that, being one with that.

Well, sometimes he gets angry and his focus is all off. There are times when he focuses on what the *other person* is doing versus on what *he* is doing; focusing on how the *other person* hits the ball versus on how *he* hits his own ball. And so he got to thinking, "*Where is my focus? Is my focus on the things that I can control or is my focus on others' things and their behavior which I have no control over? Where is my focus? Again, is it on something that I can control or is it on what the other person is doing?*"

A lot of times his thoughts, all over and over and in cycle, and in his mind there's a lot of stuck energy. And they're involved with this stuck energy as opposed to being involved with the task; the task for the team and the task for him, and that being how to get the ball over the net and in bounds! Perhaps he could quieten all these little coaching tips that are rattling around inside of him, all this debate. Quieten and see and simply look out the window and see how does the world work, how does nature work, and how do they interact with each other?

He began to think about his life and to re-sort out his life. And he thought maybe he could refrain from talking about what another is doing; instead to talk about himself and what he's doing. And the old tennis teacher thought and wished that he himself could be more genuine, could be more true versus a con; that he himself could visit with his people versus trying to put something over on them.

And the old tennis teacher, he wanted to spend his life differently. He wanted to get involved with planting of trees and flowers versus getting involved in control issues and who's in control. He was more interested in planting of trees and people hitting tennis balls and their tennis strokes, and in the red buds and the fruit and the flowers and in the azaleas versus all the control issues. He wanted to help people find their own swing, their own style, ways that they could play this game of tennis, or any game, or their life; ways to live their life.

One time he thought about two cells sitting next to each other, and these two cells communicating about the task. What is the real task and how to go about that task? He had an idea to play in a gentle manner, to live in a gentle manner, and he wished this for himself. One could think about anger, or one could think about love, and he wished in beauty may he love this. And "*In love may I sweep, and in love may I sweep this, in love I write this. There will always be anger. Okay, yet there is love deep down inside of me; and for me to focus on that love.*

CHAPTER
Three

STORY #1...simpler intentions

The Old Maintenance Man, Groundskeeper

So much of my life I've spent on trying to be someone, trying to be worthwhile, trying to get someone's attention. Whether it was a girl, possibly my parents, my father, or even to be able to cross the street. As a child, I think I had trouble crossing the street, a lot of times we would get people to help us cross the street. So, the same thing sometimes, in crossing streets and making decisions in stores, I seem to be looking for someone's attention; someone to help me, but so much also of my actions have been to be someone.

So, I've piled up positions and titles and honors, and I've done things in order to be considered for this or that. It's different from doing the job for the sake of the other person, different from doing the job for the sake of the job and what it is, different from playing for the joy of the job. No, my way of doing things, whether it was sports or different school activities, was for the glory, for the attention. It's not the same, it's for the task itself; it's not the same as following an interest. Like a Huckleberry Finn would probably follow his own interests, if he had an interest in this he would go do it. And I think those are really neat people, people who have an interest in something and they follow that. For me right now, sometimes that Chinese philosophy, that something about that book just grabs me; I have an interest in that. And I do like the drawing and I do like the people liking my drawing. I do have to get that approval; I like to get that! I don't have to get it, but I do like it.

Still, nevertheless, I can make a change in my life. I can begin to shine my own shoes, wash my own car; I can be loyal to the friends and people around me. Okay, I get nervous. I get nervous before my classes that I teach. So, I can take care and refrain from getting too tight or too loose, too tired or too hungry. I can get some rest. I can make sure I have some basic food. Okay, at times I have a hard time getting going. I can go back and focus and center on what I'm doing, on my breathing and begin to move around and massage things and warm up, and then think of it as tending to it as opposed to some production. And to see where I am, the place where I am, the task at hand where I am and the beauty where I am; I can go back to that and I can do that.

What I can control is the ball, the ball on my side of the net; control the ball. I can't control the opponent, or their personality, but what I can do is to adjust to this ball coming at me now, to either attack it or defend. What I can do is to take care of my nerves, proper rest the night before, live a simpler life, a quieter life, and think. No need to put myself in an overstressed situation; example, of my finances; example, my food or my work or doing things for admiration all the time. Instead, to function efficiently with what I have, to see the spot I'm in now, in this time and place, and to do that now.

CHAPTER
Three

STORY #2...*a new vision*

The Old Maintenance Man

Once upon a time, there was an old maintenance man, groundskeeper for an old country club. In the evening, this man taught tennis in the parks. Now, this man was beginning to want to sort out some things in his life and was coming to a time in his life when he really needed to dig in, to dig down deep and to be pure inside. It was becoming a point in time in his life when it was time for him to do this with all his might. He had his life to get on with and he needed to dig down deep to real life, to take care of him, and to take care of what he does.

Now this old maintenance man sometimes would go and he was outside so much and he saw nature and saw the trees. And once in a while, when he was just less preoccupied with his own thoughts, he would look at the trees and the nature and see them and listen, listen to the trees, to the nature, to the flowers, and to that which were his own pure thoughts. And what he thought was that often we are on a journey that he himself was on a journey. And he thought that possibly one gives as they go along this journey, as they walk along this road. Sometimes there is taking, and often this man was given to so much. And sometimes there's times when he himself gives, and this man needs to give more; to love as he goes along, to do the little things in a beautiful way, to play ball, to play his own shots.

So, the maintenance man began to look and just to see nature. And one day this owl came by and this owl and the maintenance man began to talk. It was a wise old owl. And from talking with the owl the maintenance man began to see how the grass grows, and he began to work with the grass, in accord with that in the yard; with the weeds and the little trees growing. The maintenance man began to enhance the grass as opposed to chopping it and butchering it. He began to shape the trees and the plants, to work with them according to how they were growing. The maintenance man began to look within himself and to see the courage, to face the fears that were inside of him. And in doing so, he was able to do better work to help others. His journey was now becoming an adventure.

The owl explained and taught him how he could close his eyes and see in his heart and set his heart free and let his imagination and light give way. To see in his mind's eye things that could be done, ways that classes could be taught and then become reality; to see the shot in your mind and to make that shot. The old owl helped the maintenance man and tennis player see how to play in this moment; within this point. To be able to see the shots and to go for those shots, to be free enough to let those shots evolve to come out, to be able to expand one's muscles and one's mind instead of going tight and holding the racket too tight and tightening in the strokes, to tending to each individual thing versus for the looks. Each individual character, each individual person, each individual letter as one writes something down, one letter; attend and to tend to that, to practice the serve that one would serve in the game.

The old owl encouraged the maintenance man and tennis player to take good care of himself and to trust that there will come a moment when everything that he has been taught and everything he has learned and practiced will be put into use, and to treat each person individually and each thing individually, as well as seeing the whole.

The old maintenance man began to have a new vision. He began to align himself with God, to throw in with the universe, to work with God, to walk with God, to build on the positive. He began to realize and to understand that God had a plan for him, somehow there's a plan, there's a rhythm; to go with that rhythm. He began to serve; serve the car, the rowing machine, the people, the plants, his classes, to teach sound strokes, to have a shared mission with his students. He began to contribute to the place where he worked and to the game of tennis versus for fame or for recognition, for attention or for love. The coach began to love the game and the people who played the game, and he began to love life, more so the person that was his cherished one and he only hoped what was best for her in her life instead of asking something in return.

He knew it took a whole community to develop tennis players and he simply became part of that community. He began to refrain from giving a lot of advice. Instead he simply served, got on his knees and fed balls, served balls and played his students, helping them to become who they could become. He wished for a shared mission with his students and with the people he worked for instead of performing; he would be in connection with the Earth and the Universe, with the overall Spirit in our World and Universe. In short, he began to "live in beauty" as the Navajo Indians use to describe it.

STORY #3...the circle

The Old Maintenance Man

Once upon a time there was an old maintenance man, a groundskeeper of an old country club. He helped look after the tennis courts at that country club and the people. He also taught tennis in the parks, in the evening, as well as playing tennis once in a while. This old maintenance man was beginning to get to a point in his life where he was beginning to listen to the birds, to the sounds of the birds; and even in the morning that was what helped wake him up. He would hear the sounds of the birds and began to think, "*Well maybe that's part of what life's about, to go out there and listen to the sounds of nature, the sounds that are going on out there, the song that's being played out there in nature and by God.*"

He began to see the moment as a circle. He knew that the Indians had five directions, one for north, south, east and west, and they put a color for each one of 'em; maybe a green for this and a white for this and a red and a black for this. But I know and he knew that they had a fifth direction, and that was like a big circle and it was colored green and it meant "for right now," the place where I am for right now. And so, this old maintenance man began to see time and space as circles; a circle before him where the time had come before, a circle right where he was around him where he was at this moment, and a circle for later on like it came later on.

He began to see more in the circle that he is in right now, and began to willingly accept this circle, this moment. He began to do with what he had, to love, to teach, to work in this moment. He began to thank God for the gifts that he had been given, the gift of drawing and the gift of seeing, and he really began to say, "Thank you." He wanted to do something different in his life, instead of making a fashion statement, to really do something; he wanted to build, he wanted to plant trees.

He began to see more of who he was and the gifts that he had, rather than wanting to be someone else; oh he always wanted to be someone else, to be smart like them, to have that. But he began to see a gift or two that he had and to be thankful for that. He always longed for a steady attitude. There were some things he could do to help that out; get to bed early, get to his work earlier, get to his teaching earlier, be more like a tree – centered and flexible, be a part of nature as opposed to putting his will on nature, his idea on nature, his idea on another person. But so too, as there might be a circle for this moment, there might be possibly a circle of truth for us at this moment.

So, the old maintenance man began to fashion his classes in a better way, in a way that he began to work to bring fun back to the practices; he needed to get back to that, fun for him and fun for his players. And he needed to help to fashion a class where all could contribute, that all could play, that everyone was on the team and that everyone had a chance to participate. And, he wanted to include all people in the class.

As mentioned, he began to see more of how the birds moved, and how they lived, and how the trees grew, and to begin to see again the beauty in the world, for now he was beginning to listen to life again. He had had too much baggage, too many preoccupations, too much wanting to be this or that, too many comparisons with another person, wanting what they had. His mind was clearer, he could hear what was going on, he could stop and hear what was being played in the world. He could stop and see what was evolving in the world.

And the funny thing, all of this had been going on right in front of his nose all along – all along! He had found a way to be truthful to the moment, to the circle where he was and also to be truthful and open to the bigger circle; the bigger circle of truth and movement in this world.

Three

STORY #4...*what is important*

The Old Maintenance Man

*T*his is a story of an old maintenance man who wanted to be a tennis teacher. In the morning, he helped look after the tennis courts for people at a country club. In the evening, he taught tennis. He wanted to find a way to really teach tennis and a way to change him, to change his heart, to change his life. And he wished for a beautiful lady: someone to love, someone to hold, someone to hug, someone to share his ideas, and then to listen to her. Even if he was blind, if he could close his eyes and simply listen and talk and just enjoy where he was with the person he was with, and to focus on that conversation, to give his whole attention to that conversation; to hug, to hold, to kiss.

Well, anyhow this old maintenance man, this old tennis teacher, he began to want to change his life, to change his heart; he needed to do that, to change his attitude. He began to look about this game of tennis and he had an idea that possibly you teach each person differently, each person is a different person, and that you help them find the solution that is inside of them, you work with them. And a lot of it is in little bitty things; getting back to a simpler idea, getting back to the basics. What is that? What is 'back to the basics'? But still, instead of taking their heads and opening up their heads and pouring all this information into them, it'd be helping them to come up with their solution; helping them to come up with their solutions for their shots, for their game.

One time this old maintenance man was at one of his jobs. He was parked in the parking lot, and as he looked across the field from him, he saw a lake. There was a boy pedaling a bicycle and he had a net he would catch minnows with, and possibly a fishing pole; but it was basically this boy riding his bicycle with this net to catch minnows. And it just dawned on him how simple this was; how simple this idea was; a boy going fishing.

And so, the same thing too, in our lives, this game of tennis; to keep it that simple, that basically, refreshingly simple. To look in our lives and to see the things that cross our lives each day, the little bitty things that share time with us. Whether that is a red bird or some person coming through our lives, that maybe there, there is a direction, there is a possibility for rubbing elbows and sharing ideas and coming up with a better solution or direction in our lives. To take some time to be with another person, instead of rushing here and rushing there.

You know the game of tennis itself involves playing and resting, playing and resting. He had this idea that you practice a shot that you hit to this target, and then you take the information from how that ball went towards that target. And once you've practiced this shot, then you turn it over to being quiet and trusting. If there is this picture of a stroke and there is this development of this picture of the tennis stroke and then there's the target and this hitting to this target, and then it's taking the feeling of the good shots.

Well, this old maintenance man, like he said, he needed to change his heart, he really needed to change the way he did things where he worked and the way he talked to people and the way he saw people. His whole idea in life was to be more sincere, to refrain from hiding from another person, to refrain from being coy or from hiding; just to be sincere. Being real, that's the most important thing in his life.

CHAPTER
Three

STORY #5...
to notice the clouds

The Old Maintenance Man

Once upon a time there was this old maintenance man, old and broken down. And this old maintenance man taught tennis in the evening in the parks. He was thinking about his lessons and about his life. He had an idea about his tennis lessons where he would simply meet with a person, and he would work with that person, and help that person to develop their strokes, the strokes that were inside them. Then he would learn to love seeing them get the ball over the net and inbounds, seeing them hit sound strokes, seeing the joy of that.

They would simply meet and they would play and learn, and then when their time was up; they would shake hands and they would leave. He would go his way, they would go their way. They would rest. He would simply meet; share that time and place, and play a game and learn, and then they would escape. So, he began to think a little bit about his lessons in the terms of providing ways and little games in which people could get into the game of tennis, a means to get *into* the game. Putting the ball in play is the first thing… to get the ball in so that person could get in to play and keep that ball in play, and then also a chance to escape when it's time to escape.

He even began to look at a little bigger picture. He began to look one night up at the moon and the stars, and he began to think that there is something more than what I think, and that what I am in this world; there's something bigger than me. And he began to notice that the clover is beginning to bloom and the yellow butterflies flying by and a wildflower blooming. Oh he thanked God for the clover. And he thought about running free after a ball and breathing and being able to breathe, it's something different than being too stressful. If it's too stressful then something's off. He was thankful for the clover. And he began to think about nature and God, where people were more one with God and one with nature, and to refrain from getting too tired.

About his tennis lessons, some of his fear, his biggest fear, was that he was afraid that he would fall on his face. He began to think maybe the other side of the coin was to get into the flow of it all, getting into the flow of the tennis lesson, getting into the challenge of the golf course and the conditions of the golf course. In tennis maybe the challenge of the shot, getting into the challenge of that one shot and again, the conditions that were going on; to take the ball and add some of one's own purpose to it versus contending power for power. He thought, *"Where there's fire, meet it with softness; where there is softness, meet it with hardness, instead of fire fighting fire where you have water fighting fire."*

He began to think about how the body worked and how nature works, about the rhythms, about the smoothness of nature and about motivation, how nature works, how the body works. So too in our exercise there is the flow of things; play the ball, play the course, play the flow of things, the flow of things. So activities and the activities that go with them, to see this flow and to work with this flow. He began to be thankful for his father, for his mother, for all that has been given him in his life. For the results that he's had, the good and the bad.

He began to think about service and serving the people, to pay his own bills, to be true, to play the game – the game itself. He began to look a little deeper and to think, *"Who is God bringing me in my life? Who is He bringing me? What students is He bringing to me? What are the things He's bringing to me in my life?"* His biggest thing was being out of his own moment, to be thinking somewhere else when he's really right in one place; he knew he needed to work on that, to work on serving the moment, to serving in this moment. And then once it's over with, to rest, to shake hands and to rest.

He knew he needed to be more for people, for if he was not for them who would be? He needed to be for himself, because if he was not for himself who would be? For many of his people he needed to be positive. He knew that he was on a journey as all people are on our journeys, everyone has their own journey; a journey today. He wished that he could draw what he saw, especially that which he saw was beautiful.

CHAPTER
Three

STORY #6...*simpler*

The Old Maintenance Man

*T*his is still about the old maintenance man who teaches tennis in the evenings. And he was thinking about his life and thinking about tennis and then thinking about playing sports. And on playing sports, it's about a ball game, what is a ball game? And his idea was that a person takes one shot and then another person takes it and adds their own purpose to it. That's more a give and take, a competition. One person hits it over the net; the other person takes that shot and adds a little bit of his own purpose to it. Oh yeah, some people figure out what the other person likes and dislikes and makes sure they give them what they dislike.

Now this old tennis pro, he was beginning to think about his life and his basic idea was he thought he needed to make it simpler. He needed to live his life in a simpler manner. To take one thought through till the finish, to stop setting other people straight, giving them grief. He thought that perhaps, well, he thought that he needed to go to bed earlier, to pay his bills, to teach in such a way that was non-stressful, to watch his breathing; that maybe he expected too much. He definitely believed that's how we live our lives, in the little things. For him, tennis was taking care of one point at a time, this point. Taking that point all the way through to the finish and still seeing the whole.

He was beginning to rethink his life and he needed to look into such ways that he could rethink the way he does things in his life. In his teaching he hoped to help to bring his students to their mind, to their strokes. Also, he wished to find his mind and his own strokes. He was wanting, and had one time realized, a certain sacredness of life where he was one part of a whole, and this is a certain thread, certain sacredness in this whole of life; that he was connected with this. Each person is a part of that whole and each person, if they choose, can contribute to this whole. To get back to a sense of sacredness in life, that was one of his wishes.

CHAPTER
Three

STORY #7...
Christmas an unfolding

The Old Maintenance Man

*I*t was coming to be Christmastime and the old maintenance man was beginning to think about Christmas. Christmas just started, but for him it is a year-long process of growing and living and giving. It's really something each day; it's an unfolding each day. It's more like how we live our life right now – that is what matters; the grace in which we live it, the care in which we live it.

"*This is my life*", he thought, "*I choose to live it in beauty, I choose to live it in harmony. Oh, there's no time to cry in one's beer, no time to feel sorry for one. Oh, I do feel sorry and yes, I know that, but there's no time for such, there's just too much work to do, there's plenty to focus on. There's plenty to focus on just in one's own home, one's own house. To just focus on one's own bagel; to clean up one's own car, to wax it, to sweep out the car.*" Oh, he felt good when he swept out his car. He felt good when he sewed on his own buttons. It made him feel good. He felt good to read poetry out loud.

Yes, Christmas is a year-long process, its growing and loving each day, it's how we live our life right now; that's what matters. The grace in which we live it, the care, and the care for each person that comes along our way. Oh there was a man down the street and he had only a year to live. How would he live his life? He was faced with such.

The old maintenance man again thought that the more he did for himself and for others, he felt better. What are we to do? To follow one's own dream, to follow God's plan, to follow one's star? The old maintenance man, he waited, he waited for God to come. And how does God come into our lives? "*And what do I have to give to people this Christmas? What can I give to them? Oh yes I can use a bunch of money. But is it possible that I can give to them something that I can do, something that I can draw? Is it possible to focus in my life on what I have, to be content with what I have?*" Life is short!

Is it possible to describe things as they are? To see the beauty that comes through my life, the coincidences, oh yes, keeping my eye on the ball and getting that ball back over the net and inbounds? To focus on playing versus on the winning and the losing, and to be so sad about winning and losing, but instead, to focus on this ball coming right now, this moment. Oh yes I fear it, I fear that death, I fear falling on my face. Is it possible still to see a bigger picture? To see how I can help and how people can help me and have helped me?

"*What is real?*" the maintenance man thought. And then he thought, "*It's to quiet one's mind and to see, and it is to serve, to do it; to go to work and have a clear mind, to help people. To quiet one's mind and see the little birds that come through our lives each day, and the flowers, and just to see them and to enjoy them. Oh, and if you choose to draw them… okay. You choose to describe them… okay. But first of all, simply to see them, to breathe them in and out, to let them come inside one's mind, that's enough*"

It's about quieting one's mind, quieting all the voices, the anger, the debate and seeing God's creatures. Seeing the whole evolve, seeing the people in my life now and wishing them all well and praying for them that they will all make it and live well. A simpler life, more grounded in God, more grounded in the things I can do rather than wanting something that I do not have.

CHAPTER

Three

STORY #8...tennis
a life time of learning

The Old Maintenance Man

*T*he old maintenance man began to look at his life and to see it's a time for him to change the way he is, the way he does things, to begin to see the beauty in this moment in the little things, it's how we are this day. For him it was time now in his life to use that which he has. To have his own mind there, present, to see as an artist sees, to refrain from offering too many suggestions and advice giving, to listen to people and to walk with people, to stay in the point; to go for something versus just not making errors, to build; to face himself and his own fears, to being real and regular.

For tennis, it's a lifetime endeavor; it's a game for a lifetime to play throughout ones life. And each day it's different. Each day we wake up, the angle of our racket is different; the way we play is different. We're all on this trip together; we're all on our own trip in our own game, and yet we're together. So, for him it was for him to find his own style, his own walk, to find out what he believes in and to do it, to find his own gifts and to give those gifts.

CHAPTER
Three

STORY #9...that first step

The Old Maintenance Man

*I*t's about a direction in his life, about a thread going all the way through; a simpler life, a more honest life. A lot of times he spent a lot of his time trying to impress others doing things for the opinion of the coach, for the evaluation given by the coach versus playing and taking care of what one was doing, versus playing for the sake of playing. Everything depended upon the evaluation from the coach. He's also tried to control others thoughts. He needs to stop that, trying to control another's way they do things; instead to play his own checker, to play his own shot.

Yes, he's looking for a simpler life. Sometimes things are just overwhelming and he's very easily overwhelmed. A simpler life; in his food, his going to bed earlier, his walking, his running, his playing, the way he talks. Less doubt, less pity, less fat, less baggage; quiet instead, see things as they are instead. And, if he's lucky, to see the birds that come into his life, to see the moment, the coincidences, the preciousness of this moment. He thought, "*I'm simply gonna live and let the chips fall where they may, you know, it's my soul; simply live. And as far as tennis, to serve my students, to look and see which enfolds that day; for the universe is my university.*"

He thought it was time now to prepare for God, time to get ready for Jesus, for it is Christmastime. Perhaps there'll be a miracle today. Even if it's not even Christmastime it's just time to go to Mass. Perhaps today there'll be a miracle and that he will be able to change his life, to start anew, a new life tonight and to see that which enfolds, to see that which is right in front of him. There are no great pressing things to do. It's in the little things. And tonight his present is how he lives his life in the present. "*That's my present*", he thought, "*in how I live my life in this present.*"

Sometimes he has a hard time getting going, getting started. Maybe that's the beauty of tennis, to simply get involved in running after that little ball, chasing that ball and taking it and adding some more purpose to it; one's own purpose. Still getting involved in the running after the ball, getting involved and doing something for another person and the bravery that comes out of that love for that other person. And now; this has sometimes helped him make that first step. Sometimes it's a matter of going to the bathroom, sometimes it's in biological needs and sometimes it's a matter of possibly that centering versus looking too far down the road.

CHAPTER
Three

STORY #10...the bigger plan

The Old Maintenance Man

He had an idea that tennis is a part of life; it's a part of the unfolding of life, of the mystery. His idea was to play the ball, that each point is important. Every day is important! This task facing me right now is important. There's a circle right in front of me now; it helps to define where I am now. Tennis can be about playing the person. So it is with a game of playing the ball, and it can be a game of playing the person. Sometimes it's a game within a game. Better to see the real game.

Where do our nerves come from? Well sometimes it's from thinking of things being too much, too big a deal, and this adds a little extra nerves, too big of nerves. The nerves help get us going, they help start the engine. But sometimes we can make too much of something and make it all be too big. One idea is to do what I do and to get it before it becomes an emergency.

Maybe, it's we get too much, make too big a deal, and we want to be a great writer or do great art versus doing service. Maybe it's photographing one flower, drawing one simple flower. And besides, it's neither up nor down, it's sideways, it's what it reminds me of. So any comments like that are neither up nor down, it's more sideways; it's a better way to play. In all of this, every bit of this is really about how that maintenance man can grow to become the person that he is, the person he's to become; for there's something bigger than all of this, and all this pettiness and contending for power and controlling. Who is the boss? Who's not the boss? And there's something bigger, there's a bigger plan in life and it's where we all push for that life, for that bigger plan. We all have a part in that bigger plan, and to tie into that versus thinking of all these petty little bitty things here, to get into that bigger focus that bigger picture of life.

CHAPTER
Three

STORY #11... an
unfolding of the Mystery

The Old Maintenance Man

*N*ow this old maintenance man, he wanted to get back on track. He wanted to get back on his breathing, his writing, his drawing and back on the focus of his life. So much of what his life was about how people grow and developed as a people. He was very interested in how people grow and develop to become human beings, and about how they learned and played and worked. This was what he was interested in. You know in his own particular life, he knew he had to begin taking care of the little things. He needed to pay his own bills; he needed to become responsible for his own actions.

He one time heard a quotation, "Begin, and the conditions you will need will come to you." *"If I go beyond what I have",* he thought, *"I'm doing too much. It's wrong to put so much or to go past such, beyond to go past this one page even."* He knew that he had a course and he hoped that he had a course in life and that everyone has a course that they're gonna run. That there's a time to mend, yes, and there's a time to do. He knew he was afraid of dying; yes, he was afraid. And he had some problems with his arm, like in hitting tennis balls. He wanted to find a way that felt good for his arm. He started thinking about his health and about his life and he thought, *"slow and easy, let everybody else go fast";* he would take it slow and easy. And his walk and his play would be gentle, no need to overdo it.

A lot of times he would simply see something beautiful and take a picture of it and do what he could to draw it or to talk about it to describe that. And even that was too much. He simply needed to really just see it and enjoy it as it was. He was beginning to give thanks to God for the talents that he was given; the ability to draw, it was a wonderful talent.

He was looking for a simpler life. He felt that if he could clear his mind, he could then possibly help others. He thought it would be important to do as many things as he could for his own self and to complete those projects. He thought it would be important to go and see the world, to go and see how it unfolds, how each day there's an unfolding. So, when the light comes and the birds begin to sing, they're talking about this unfolding each day of that Mystery of life. He wished he could have peace in this moment, may he be in peace in each moment, as many moments as he can in his life.

For God knows what he's doing, He knows why He's done what He's done; He has a reason. He hoped that he could keep his head above the water, so he could see this great Mystery unfolding each day, so he could see this sacred journey that he was going on; although, he didn't really know for sure where he was going and where it would take him, but he would at least be cognizant of the journey enfolding each day. And it'd be a journey into the weave of life versus an alarm going off and shattering early in the morning, it would be a journey into the weave of life.

He wished that he could be quieter and purer and more sincere in how he did things with himself and with others. That he would be real, that he would pay his bills, and he would just live within himself and play within himself rather than overextending. And that he would play and walk and work in a gentler manner, as well as teach, and that he would give up all his biases with all of his bosses and just get back down to serving and loving and listening and following. These were his wishes.

CHAPTER
Three

STORY #12...a path to follow

The Old Maintenance Man

He was beginning to think about getting back to basics, back to sound strokes; it was time for him to get back. And he was thinking about being in harmony with the trees, with the clouds, with the wind, with nature. There's something called "nature's time", nature's cycle, nature's rhythm, "nature's time", and being in step with that, in tune with that, with "nature's time."

He wondered why God had put him here on this earth. What was His reason why He had placed him here? And once in a while, he'll see that there is a reason why God has put him here. He needs to see more of that. For the time being though, it's for him to dig in, to take dead aim at his target. It's one shot at a time, to hit solid shots to the targets, to play the game. And for him, to see what brings contentment and clarity and peace; that is the path for him to follow.

CHAPTER
Three

STORY #13...
purposes and wishes

The Old Maintenance Man

He started looking about the way he did things and he wanted to stop conning people. He wanted to be at work early, to stick with his people and to look after himself. He knew that he needed to work on things such as silence and love and reverence, generosity, courage and chastity; that great minds have purposes, others have wishes.

CHAPTER

four

$\mathcal{STORY}\#$ *1...change*

The Old Maintenance Man, Groundskeeper

Once upon a time, there was an old maintenance man who worked at an old country club. This maintenance man wanted to be a tennis player. The maintenance man took care of the tennis courts at this old country club and he taught tennis in the evenings in the parks. But still, he wanted to become a tennis player himself. He wanted to become a real tennis player. And he wanted to change his life around; it was time for him to change his life.

There was an arch at this country club and he had this idea that, if he could, just walk through this arch and when he came out the other side; he would be changed. He would change his life just like that with the snap of a finger, in a voluntary manner. He could change, and that's what he chose; he chose to change his life. He will have to do a different way; he'd have to rethink his life and to rethink it in a big way, in a big time way. He wanted to refrain from being a conman himself to con people. He wanted to be true and sincere to people, and he wanted to learn how to play this game of tennis.

He thought he needed first of all, a solid base, to establish a solid base when he played tennis. And then once he saw his opportunity, he saw a hole, then he would go for that hole; he would hit his ball to that hole. Or sometimes, he would create an opening, or sometimes, he thought he would see where the person plays, see where they like to play and what they like to do and where they are comfortable. Once you can establish this, where their ways of hitting the ball are comfortable and where their preference is; then he thought he could pull them out of that territory and help get them in a territory where they were not comfortable.

Oh, this old maintenance man, he knew he really had a task ahead of him. And that task was for him, he himself, to always keep his eye on the endeavor at hand, the task at hand. He had a tendency to take his eye off that endeavor. Constantly in his life he had to redefine, "*What is that task? What is the main thing that we're doing right here? What is the spirit of what we're doing?*" In his work he thought, "*Well that's to take care of these people and to take care of these courts and these grounds; that's my task when I'm at work.*"

The old maintenance man had an idea. He wanted to see a bigger picture versus this person or that person. He wanted to see a bigger picture in what he was doing and that he's caring for people. This old maintenance man, he needs to serve, serve his people and to serve in the game of tennis; to roll the dice and see what happens; to serve and let it go where it goes; to refrain from putting oneself in a poor position first. He thought, "*To serve a bigger picture and to thank God for the things that I can do, for at least there are some things that I can do, and to thank God for that*".

So the old maintenance man, he began to learn and to read how to center himself, how to become more like a tree and become grounded, to center oneself instead of being so overextended. He learned to keep his eyes on that task at hand, on that ball, and on playing that ball, and on the game. Oh that centeredness! That centeredness is also a sense of being in harmony versus out of harmony. The old maintenance man began to think that he himself needed to rethink his whole life in terms of harmony, in terms of overextending, in terms of keeping his eye on the task, in terms of working for the whole; to serve, to serve in the game of tennis and to serve in the game of life, to get involved with that, with the serving.

The old maintenance man began to think about the word "Emmanuel" meaning, 'the Emmanuel within him,' God within him. He began to stop and to see people and see the beauty in people. He even thought he would like to draw that if he could. But if nothing else, he began to stop and to see the beauty. The old man began to serve those people today. He began to get on his knees and to serve.

So much of the time he would end up giving himself the short end of the stick versus setting up a winning situation; set up a position. And he would play games at times when it was not a time to play games. And then, he would not play the game when it was time to play the game. There's a time to play games and there's a time to be true and to work.

The old man began to look at things and he thought about having a purpose and a purpose as a goal, a destination to go to. And then, there's the how, the way of walking, of locomotion to get to that goal, a way of traveling, keeping one's mind on the task till the finish. There's an overall ratio of work and rest and work and rest, and one needs to honor this ratio, this work/rest ratio.

The old man began to take care of each moment, each moment taking care of the task at hand. He refrained from overextending himself instead he returned back to the center and he returned back to the true center, that of serving other people and himself and serving God. He began to look at his balance both psychologically and physically in harmony. He began at times to see through the eyes of the other person. And most of all, he began to see the beauty that was already there right where he was, versus trying to take something and make it beautiful. He began just to see and to accept the beauty that was there, of the trees, the plants that were already growing there.

Oh yes, he always needed a solid base, a center, a steadiness, that of like a rock, or even better, like a willow tree that blows and changes with the wind and moves back to the center, that adapts with the wind. He always needed to keep his eye on the task at hand. He began to see, *"Hey look, let's stop all this power struggle, let's get away from being so locked into who's the boss, who's controlling and the power struggle"*. Instead, he began to care for the person and sometimes he wanted to draw that which was beautiful, a drawing of something that was beautiful and a drawing of the things that came across his life that day, a flower, a tree, a leaf. And he began to think of drawing the Whole of life.

On that day the old maintenance man, he picked up his wheelbarrow and he pushed, and he pushed it through that arch, and when he came out he had changed. He'd changed his life around, because he wanted to change it, he chose to change it. He made up his mind that he would change his life.

CHAPTER

four

STORY# 2...in Harmony

The Old Maintenance Man, Groundskeeper

Once upon a time, there was an old maintenance man who worked at an old country club. He took care of the tennis courts at this old country club and he was getting broken down and worn out. He was thinking, he had heard a program on TV, and he was beginning to think about an idea. And this is how the idea was going around in his mind, and what he was beginning to think about.

He began to think about the cell, about the human cell, and how each human cell has a chance to right itself; to maintain a certain amount of balance. Built in within each human cell in life, the very basic building blocks of life, there are mechanisms in which that cell: can help protect itself; can help reproduce; can help carry out certain functions, normal functions, that are just built right within the cell itself; and certain ways to heal itself, as it was said on TV that night.

And the idea was that if we could find out or work with those healing systems within the body, that the body has certain systems in which to help heal. If we could get connected to that and tie in to those things, it would be a better way to work with people in a medical way; a better way to live. We could even start this ahead of time. We could start at the very beginning and what we eat before at the very beginning can help us to maintain our wellness. In the way we go to sleep in the night, the earlier in the night, the peacefulness as we go to sleep can help maintain our wellness, our wholeness.

And yes, a certain amount of movement, stretching, and flexibility can help us play throughout our entire life, so that our life will be a life during our lifetime, as much as possible. That our life could possibly be a game throughout our life, a play throughout our life, a work throughout our life; that we could continue throughout our life, the best we can.

He also had been thinking a lot about breathing. How breathing in itself, learning to breathe deep down deep beneath the belly button can help a person really get into some states of energy that he's never had before that help him relieve some of that tension that sometimes we choke in our mouths and in the top part of our bodies. The cell is more here and now versus looking ahead. Breathing, coming back to this moment, breathing in, breathing out; focusing more on this moment as opposed to looking down the road. That's where the tension sometimes comes, this looking down the road, this worry. So, he began to think about these things and he began to focus more on the whole; seeing things as a whole, seeing balance, and to do things to get the healing process going and to stay going if we can do that in our lives. Find certain ways that we can get this healing process going.

Now this old man, used to be a young man; both young and old. Anyhow, this young man and old man, this man he plays tennis and he sees tennis and teaches tennis. And he began to think of his game, the game of tennis, as a whole. And as far as concentration, if one could focus on the whole versus so much on the parts, but to keeping a focus on this whole. So this is what he was beginning to think about; this wholeness, this balance, and maintaining balance, at least a striving for balance. Yes, often we're turned upside down and then we want to right ourselves, learning to be flexible enough to come back to balance, to come back to the center.

Well, this old maintenance man, he works outside a lot and he's fortunate enough to be outside and to see nature, to be around nature. And although he's often preoccupied in his mind with all these ideas, once in a while he'll stop and look up and see nature. And he was wondering, *"What if we could stop and see the way things are in the world? To see the way nature works. The way the* trees work, the way the rain washes away the film and cleanses the earth and washes away one's soul and bathes one's soul. To see the way the trees grow and develop and move, and why some grow and some do not grow, and why some become tall and some not. To see how flowers are able to raise themselves up even though when they are in almost impossible conditions, but they're still able to find their way through that little crack and grow; and to see a blue jay taking a bath in the rain." Well, he began to look at nature and, "If we could see just what is going on."

And he began to see not only that, he began to see the way things are, but he also began to think about, "Hey! What are the gifts that I have? What are the things that are given to me in my life?" This old maintenance man wanted to give something to the world; he wanted to make a gift. And I guess when it boils down to it, everybody has certain gifts. When he could, he just needed to give what he could give, to give his talents, and that's what he wanted to do in life. He wanted to form his own identity, an identity with nature, an identity with the community, with life, but still his own identity.

He began to realize that life is precious, the preciousness of life. And he began to realize that his gift would be in how he does the things in his life. The little way that he does the things in his life, that could be his gift. He once in a while will take stock of them in his life and see what God gave him, certain things to be thankful for, certain talents and gifts. He hopes to be able to use those, to find those, to realize those things. He began to think, "This is my life. These are my people." And as he went through his life, he wanted to give a little bit to each person in his life, especially to his people.

He also came back to thinking that one of the reasons he had somehow ended up in this job as a maintenance man, was that he himself needed that; he himself needed to work on that one thing in his life. To maintain things: to maintain his own life, to sew on the buttons, to clean out his car, to shine his shoes, and to rake his leaves. And even further, he needed to prevent some things before they started happening. So there's a reason why he is where he is in life and he's beginning to see this and to understand this and accept this. No, there's not going to be nothing great, but if he can only pay his bills and if he can do the job that he's supposed to be doing; that's a good start. That's a plenty good start, to be honest and be truthful, and pay without cheating people; and to finish what he starts; when he starts something, to finish it.

He's beginning to realize it's how he goes about his life, his job; that that can be his gift. It's how he does what he does right here in his job, that that can be his masterpiece, his art, his story, his gift. And, he can do that by getting in touch with the system that already exists in the body, the system of nature, the system of healing, and the way that nature works, which is already in his body, and which is all around him, all the time. Just get in touch with that, not just, but to take that, to get in touch with that harmony within himself and within nature and within the whole community. Get in touch with the bigger picture of what God wants, to be in harmony with that, to quietly be in harmony with that. There's no way he can do anything and everything that everybody wants. But he can possibly get in harmony with those basic things and plod along doing the job at hand, the task at hand; giving to the world, to the universe.

CHAPTER
Four

$STORY$ #3...*the leaves*

The Old Maintenance Man, Groundskeeper

One time, there was an old maintenance man who worked in an old country club. Now one time during lunchtime, he was asked to watch the shop while other people went to lunch. And as he was watching the shop and sitting in the back room looking through the window out towards the trees and the parking lot and the flowers and the plants, he started watching the leaves on the tree and the wind blowing through those leaves. The wind was going through the leaves and the leaves stayed on, they were in harmony, they were being blown and they moved back and forth. They were holding on, the leaves were staying on; it was not their time to go. Then there goes one, there goes one leaf; it goes to make its flight to the earth.

And the maintenance man thought about that flight; that flight of that leaf on as it went down and waved and turned and fell to the earth and landed on the earth. And he thought about that leaf, *"Is that it? Is that all that leaf has lived for; this one particular flight; this one particular graceful move and tumble down to the earth? Or was it about what went on before in that leaf's life: the first initial budding, the first initial leaves coming out? And then the fuller leaves or where will the leaves go once they go to the ground? They'll be raked up, bagged, and put in the dumpster? Or will they be cut up and spread out and go into making grass and soil for the grass and the flowers and other trees?"* Here is this leaf, where would you want to go? In the dumpster, or back into the yard to be turned into soil so that other plants can grow?

Perhaps there's something bigger. Perhaps there's a task at hand, a bigger task, and this leaf is part of this bigger task. There is a God, something bigger than just this life. And, He's got some plan, and this particular leaf is part of that overall plan. And again, if you were that leaf what would you rather do; be raked up and bagged up and put into the dumpster? Oh, maybe yes, again you'll be made into soil; it'll go into a landfill. Or would you like to be chopped up and spread back out onto the soil to let the soil grow to have a chance to have some kind of nutrition, to grow and to bring another flower or tree into being, and to give some food for another animal and something beautiful for some human to see? Would it like to protect others from the sunshine, or to become a home for some animal to live, or to give a bird refuge from the rain?

STORY# 4...tennis
as an adventure

The Old Maintenance Man, Groundskeeper

O nce there was an old maintenance man who worked at an old country club and he helped take care of the tennis courts and the surrounding grounds. He also taught tennis in the evening in the parks. His life was around the game of tennis. And he began to think about this game of tennis, especially in terms of one of his students. In this particular idea about tennis, he began to think of tennis as an adventure. *"What if we began to think of tennis as an adventure and a game versus being a drill? To hit so many down the lines and so many cross courts, and to push and pull and shove and cajole this person to hitting these particular shots; to forcing your ideas on these shots and your ideas on this particular person. What if somehow we could lead this person, lead this student in a game? Then, it would be a game, an adventure, just like board games and into life games."*

Then he began to think that that adventure, the real adventure, is outside. It's out here rather than always inside of oneself; it's an adventure to go to. And he began to think that some of the adventure in life is to stop and see the beauty that's right around oneself. To listen to the sounds of the country club, the sounds of the people playing tennis. To see the beauty around the tennis courts as well as what is going on the court itself.

And then he began to think about how sometimes people will tell a story, tell their story of their adventure. They tell their own story or sometimes we borrow other people's stories to live in their adventure. The telling of a story; telling and describing of what we have seen that day in our journeys, to describe what we saw in our journey today, to be thankful for what we've had, to being able to see, to hear, to taste, to smell, to be around.

Sometimes the old maintenance man began to be able to draw as a way of describing what he saw that day. Once in a while, he was lucky, he was very fortunate to see some of his drawings in his workplace. People had put the drawings on their desks. A person had put their drawing on his desk. It made him very humble. It almost made him want to work harder. It helped him, seeing his work, his drawings, displayed there in his own workplace; it made him very humble and even feel more a part of the place.

CHAPTER

four

STORY# 5...*one's true self*

The Old Maintenance Man, Groundskeeper

Once upon a time there was this old maintenance man who worked at an old country club and he used to take care of the tennis courts and the surrounding grounds. He also taught tennis in the evenings in the parks. And he was thinking one day, he was beginning to think, *"Where is one's truth, one's true self? Is it for doing things for them or for the fame and the glory? And what am I doing in the things I do? Am I doing it for them, for that person, for those people, for those students, for the people I work for? Or am I doing it to achieve fame and glory? Am I doing it out of love and to be at peace with that person, or am I doing it to make a point, to impress?"*

He wanted to begin to find activities in his life that he was doing where there is peace. Where, when he goes about his life, he is in peace, and he's giving peace to other people, rather than ragging them. So, he was beginning to think about how he needs to live in harmony with life rather than against life, and how he could live in harmony with life, with God, with nature, versus against life, running against the ways of life and the processes of life. And he began to think, *"Is what we put into it what we're going to get out? So, if we put in grief, we're going to get out grief. If we put in peace, we have a better chance to get out peace. Put in some harmony at the beginning, we have a better chance to have harmony come out at the end. Put out love at the beginning, we have a better chance to have some love come out at the end."*

Four

STORY# 6...a match

The Old Maintenance Man, Groundskeeper

*T*he old maintenance man had some personal thoughts on himself. They were; "*It's time to stop using people, it's time, myself, to tend to that which is in front of me; to make my own bed. It's how one sets up one's own life.*" He said that he could change; he thought that he could change his life. "*There's no need for me to live my life the way other people live.*" He also thought it'd be, for himself, "*To go ahead and to quietly work, to work on what I have. So much of this hatred and anger and stuff is about control and about not having control. There's some things you have no control over. Sometimes you're fighting in a controlled drama, a conflict about control. Sometimes, and when we are in situations, we're really like gypsum, we wash out. No, for me, it's for me to live within my means. It's best to refrain from overextending myself. To do the job, to refrain from getting bent out of shape; that's it, that it's a game. To deal with what I have to deal with.*"

He thought, "*For example, these tennis courts; it's focusing more on the ball that has been given to me to play, the ball on my side of the court, and for me to get this ball back over the net. Then the other person takes the ball and, therefore, that's for them to deal with and for them to get it back over the net. It's fun when you can take it and then add a little bit of your own purpose to it, your own intention to it. They can take it and add a little bit of their own intention to it, and then it becomes a freer match, a freer situation.*"

CHAPTER
four

$\mathcal{STORY}$# 7...*taking*
stock of himself

The Old Maintenance Man, Groundskeeper

*T*he idea was to stop and to see Christmas and to begin to think of Christmas as a beginning rather than an ending. It starts with Christmas Day, and then with each day it unfolds, almost like a child with each day grows a little bit more, learns a little bit more, and their life unfolds; they explore, they see the world, they learn. Well so too, in Christmas. A lot of times this could be a beginning, and with each day after Christmas there is an unfolding, a more of a realizing the meaning of Christmas in our lives. It's a time to stop and to think back over this year, and to think about this year and the different things that have happened this year, and to be thankful for those things. It's time to stop and think to remember this year.

"Life goes so fast that we forgot. We forgot about the tennis courts and how they were changed. We forgot about my father's operations (he had three operations this past year); about my own operation and taking care of myself; about the kids in the summertime and the playing in the summertime; about the students that I've had through the year; and all the different things that have happened this past year. It's about a purpose. It's good to have a purpose in life. To have a job, to go check on that job, a place to go, a place to go check on, a place to have one's own purpose. So that's where I think it's important."

"If one could set up their lives so that they always have this chance to go and see, to go and to do, to go and check on, to help prepare; they have a purpose. Whether they're helping prepare a person to play the game of tennis, helping prepare the courts so people can come and play, that they're drawing, describing, seeing the world as it is; they have a place to go. It's neat. And that would be something to work towards, to see, to describe what I see, versus to set the world straight. To personally calm down, to center; this is one of my personal wishes."

So the young man, the maintenance man, now the old man, began to stop finally and to see the world as it was in front of him; the one that was right in front of him, right now. And he stopped making so many suggestions to the world, so much advice-giving. He wanted to stop that in his life; instead, to fix, to help fix things up. To stop to see nature as it is, to see the whole, to do things so the body can be whole and the mind whole, so it can function better; that there is change in life. That's one of the things that there's always going to be, there's always going to be change. It's never going to be just perfect and status quo, there always will be change. It's time to stop, to think, to pray, to be able to thank, possibly to give a modest gift to the world.

The young man wanted to give a modest gift. He wanted to have a purpose in his life. He wanted, for his life, he wanted to be able to make his life sacred; that there be a sacred thread throughout his life to God, and to nature, to himself, and to the world. It was almost like he wanted to make his life like a prayer, a sacred life, and build back up. He would like to do something out of caring for someone versus for fame, to love these people. He's finding out that it's exciting to find out that there is something inside of him that he didn't know he had; for example his ability to draw.

And as far as his people, he began to think, *"Hey! It's these people that are right in front of me right now, right before me. It's so hard with one's own parents. But at least I can do it with these people that are right in front of me, and maybe I can be just a little bit better with my own parents."*

He wanted to give something very beautiful to the world; to walk, to stop and see the world. And he knew that he needed to finish that which he had started. That all said and done, all of these ideas are wonderful but he needs to finish that which he has started, to complete.

STORY# 8...
taking stock further

The Old Maintenance Man, Groundskeeper

*T*he old maintenance man began to stop and to think and to look back on his life and see where he needed to say, "Thanks." It was a time to take stock of his life, a time to help chart his course; a direction for the future. He began to look back on his life, and he began to say, "*Hey, it's time to stop and to thank, a time to mend, a time to shine my shoes, to sew on the buttons, a time to stop and to be thankful for what I have, to be thankful for my health, for my parents' health, to think back on this year and think of all the things in my life, and to be thankful, to begin to think on how I can help where I am now.*"

He began to think about teaching tennis, about leading people to their swing, and about hearing their story. He even began to see for a moment what this country club was all about. He saw people meeting and greeting in the parking lot and then hugging. It's about hugging, this country club.

He began to see the leaves sail down from the trees. He began to say, "hello" and asking for nothing in return, simply a "hello." He looked at this time as a time to rest, a time to serve, a time to be in harmony, in balance, to be whole. He began to think about how to live, how to work, how to play in harmony with nature, with ourselves, with God. It was a time to be a part of nature, part of God, within God, and God within us. It was a time to be in harmony, to get the little steps in order from the very beginning. The maintenance man began to keep his eye on the ball, on the task at hand instead of making fun of people. He began to see that, yes, there is change and to go with that change, to be flexible enough to move with the changes. He began to go and to see, to visit and to enjoy. He began to see clearer the task at hand. And he knew he needed to get back to that, back to the task at hand that is in front of him. Yes, it was a time to mend, a time to enjoy.

He wanted, and he knew it was for him, to teach the people who came into his life, to work with the people who came into his life. He wanted to draw what he saw come into his life. He wanted to listen; to really listen to another. It was different from using a person; it was different from using a person in order to go up the ladder. It was, instead, to attend to the task at hand; to tend to this ball coming at me right now; and together to find some meaning in this world.

He began to think, *"How do I want to live my life? Instead of dancing around something versus really grasping it, to see the world, to give myself in service to the task at hand, but how? How can I be willing to be open, about being very sound first, and about doing? What am I doing? I'm giving my life, to give my life for a friend."*

And he began to think also, in terms of the other person, of what's good for them from their point of view. *"It's beginning to take care of someone for the sake of them. It's taking care of the little things, such as washing my car, cleaning my house; the basic things first. And then to serve, that my place is to serve. The reason I'm here is really to serve. And then I must draw my motivation from something other than my promotion; my ego must be out of this. No one owns anyone or anything. The thing is to serve."*

Now the old maintenance man was thinking about a lot of these things. And one day when he was watching the shop and thinking about his life, when he was really particularly confused with his life: he opened up this little book. The page that came open was a quotation which said, "See for yourself what brings contentment and clarity and peace. This is the path for you to follow." And this is the path this young man began to think about, as a way to chart his course, his own course in life.

And he began to see the leaves falling to the ground, and he began to see his part in the whole scheme of things; to see that part and to do that part.

Four

STORY# 9...ideas
from his racket bag

The Old Maintenance Man, Groundskeeper

The old maintenance man went through his old tennis racket bag, the one he uses as his teaching bag; his bag of tricks. As he plays tennis and practices his tennis before his classes, a lot of times he has some ideas. After he teaches a class, he grabs a piece of paper out of this old racket bag and he writes his idea down and stuffs it back into the bag. Well every so often, he cleans out his racket bag, and that's what he did the other day and that's what he did today. He cleaned out that bag and he pulled out those notes and he began to look at the notes to see what he has been thinking about this past year. This is what he found.

He said, *"He thought first that tennis is simply a game, that he had an idea to treat each class as a game. You spin the racket. You shake hands when it's over. A lot of the game is a process, versus the outcome. The outcome is where you win or lose, the scorekeeping, the score of the game, the result. The process is how you get to that spot; how you travel; the process of learning, the process of playing; the playing of the game. To be involved in the process, versus being concerned so much with the outcome."*

On his serve, he began to think about his own serve. He would like to serve like the wind, like the trees, like the clouds. He you would like to make himself like a tree, flexible and nimble. He would serve with the wind, and feeling the wind on your face and making the ball go with the wind. He would be looking up to the clouds and serving and stretching up to the clouds. He wondered if he could make himself like these elements at times, that you would be sincere about how you strike the ball and how you play the game.

He thought it would be best to cut all the suggestions and advice-giving; less talk, but instead to quietly focus on the ball. He thought it would be good to feel his own feet on the floor, on the earth, on the court. To be aware of your earth, your surroundings, until you feel quiet and composed, then you walk, then you serve, then you move. When you walk, you just walk. When you run, you simply run. He thought it'd be best in this class, what he would like to do and refrain from doing, instead of conning them. Instead, see the way things really are. He wanted to teach according to the way things are in nature, the way people move, the way people really do move. To begin to take care of people, and chat when it's time to chat, and to be quiet when it's time to be quiet.

He began to look at his own life and his own game. It's in how we strike the ball in our lives; it's how we play the game. It's about getting that serve in. It's about getting into the game, the game of life. He began to think it's about making peace with himself and peace with others. It's time to make peace with his people. Okay, they have limits. Somehow you wish they would be more in this particular area but it's just not there right now. So make peace with that; that they give what they can give, and you give what you could give. And that's just the way it is and was. If you could have given better, you would have given better. But right now it's all a reaction. So instead just make peace with this and make peace with oneself and peace with others. No need more to cajole or suggest anything.

He thought, "*I want to be real, to be sincere in my life, to serve because I like to serve. There is a particular serve that I like in tennis, because I like the feel of that serve; that's my serve. That's the serve I like to do; get the ball in play and get into the game and everybody can get into the game. Meanwhile, I must keep my eye on the ball and keep working. It's healthier to run and to breathe. That's why we're here in this game; and to play a game. It's a game. We get a chance to run, to breathe, to exercise, to have activities, to rest, to play, to be with other people, and we have a chance to play a game. I want to focus on the ball and what I'm doing with the ball.*

That is the beauty of this game. In my case it's the game of tennis. It's also the beauty of other games.

Thank you.

E. C.

About the Author

E. C. helps maintain tennis courts, particularly green clay tennis courts. In the evenings he teaches tennis in the parks. He teaches primarily beginner children and adults. He has enjoyed singing in his church choir.

.... in harmony with the

flow of life.

... the Body of Christ

... Perhaps it is we ...

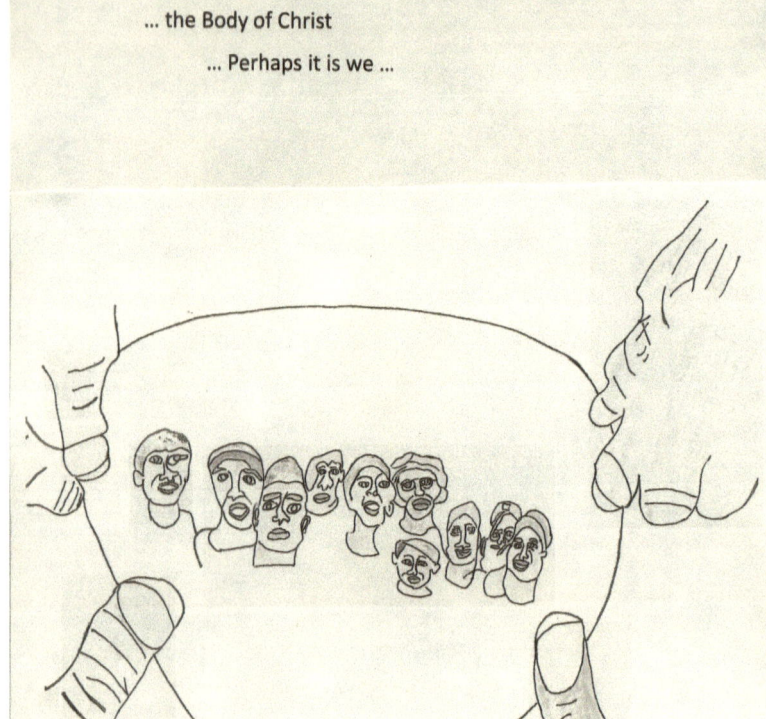

What is important?

... the affirming of life

... that is important

Life affirming life.

The game starts with love and patience and ends with love and patience...And some play all shots in between with love and patience.

In Beauty may my mind be one with God and may I bring my mind to this point.

... a connecting with the Flow of Life.

How... by quietening and see nature as it is.

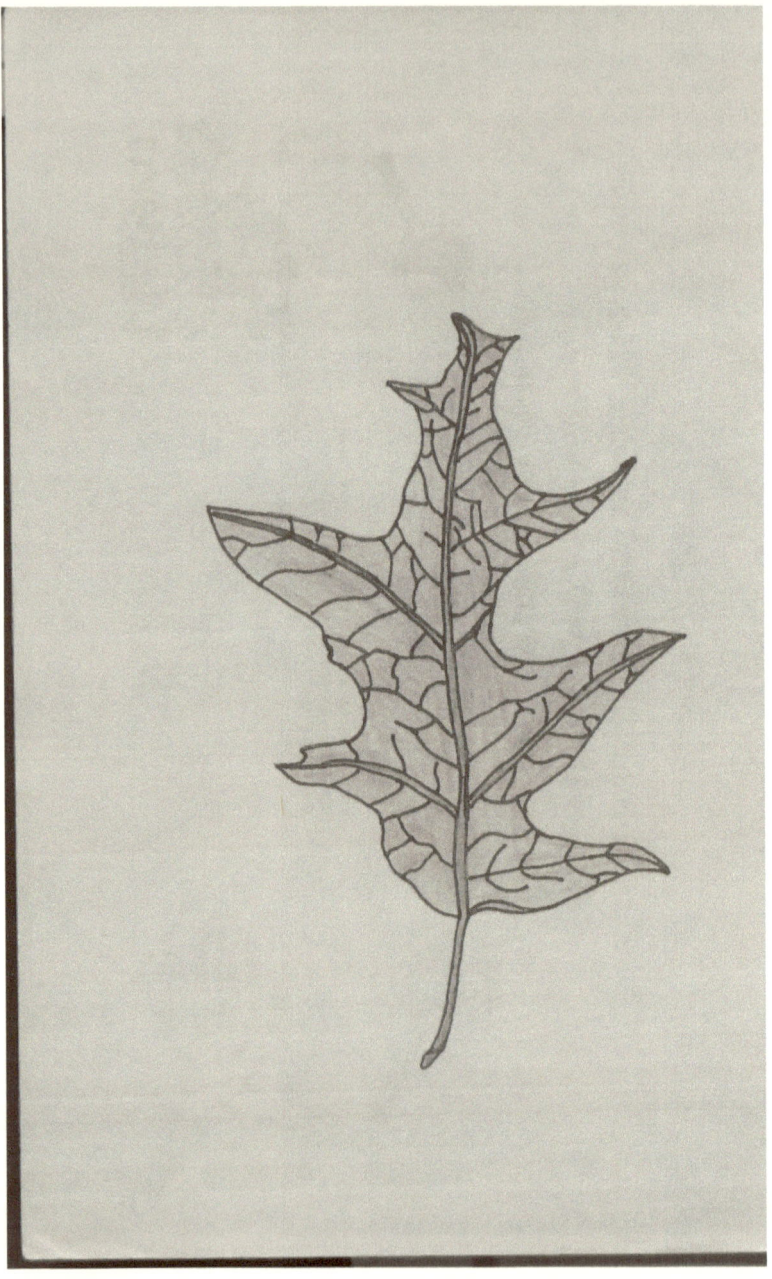